CAN WE PUT AN END TO SWEATSHOPS?

"New Democracy Forum operates at a level of literacy and responsibility which is all too rare in our time." —John Kenneth Galbraith

Other books in the NEW DEMOCRACY FORUM series:

CAN WE PUT AN END TO SWEATSHOPS?

ARCHON FUNG, DARA O'ROURKE, AND CHARLES SABEL

FOREWORD BY MEDEA BENJAMIN

EDITED BY JOSHUA COHEN AND JOEL ROGERS
FOR *BOSTON REVIEW*

BEACON PRESS
BOSTON

BEACON PRESS
25 Beacon Street
Boston, Massachusetts 02108-2892
www.beacon.org

Beacon Press books
are published under the auspices of
the Unitarian Universalist Association of Congregations.

05 04 03 02 01   8 7 6 5 4 3 2 1

This book is printed on acid-free paper that meets the uncoated paper
ANSI/NISO specifications for permanence as revised in 1992.

Composition by Wilsted & Taylor Publishing Services

Library of Congress Cataloging-in-Publication Data
Can we put an end to sweatshops? / Archon Fung, Dara O'Rourke, and
Charles Sabel ; edited by Joshua Cohen and Joel Rogers for Boston
Review.
        p.   cm. — (New democracy forum series)
Includes bibliographical references.
     ISBN 0-8070-4715-5
  1. Sweatshops.   2. Sweatshops—Prevention.   I. Fung, Archon, date   II.
O'Rourke, Dara.   III. Sabel, Charles F.   IV. Cohen, Joshua, date   V.
Rogers, Joel, date   VI. New democracy forum.
     HD2337.C36 2001
     331.25—dc21

                                                        2001003953

CONTENTS

FOREWORD

MEDEA BENJAMIN

In the 1960s and 1970s, when first world corporations began to close their own factories and contract their products from factories overseas, saving money was certainly foremost on their minds. After all, how can you compare the cost of a product made by an American earning eight dollars an hour with one made by an Indonesian earning twenty cents an hour? The potential savings were enormous.

But companies realized another major advantage by contracting out the work instead of manufacturing themselves: they could divest themselves of the pesky problem of dealing directly with workers. Gone were the old-fashioned worries of how to keep your workforce union-free or lower your payroll taxes. No need to haggle with workers over maternity benefits or sick leave. In the brave new world of corporate-led globalization, you might have to bribe a foreign official here and there to grease the wheels of a business venture, but dealing directly with workers became someone else's headache. That also freed up companies to put their energies where the potential payoff was the greatest: marketing.

Nike became the poster child for this new-age company where the product itself was somewhat incidental. Nike owned no factories at home or overseas but purchased millions of pairs of shoes from Asian factories. So uninterested was CEO Philip Knight in these overseas factories and workers that he never even bothered to visit the countries—Indonesia, China, and Vietnam—where Nike was setting up shop. Nike did, however, put billions of dollars into selling a lifestyle, a brand name, a logo. The swoosh became ubiquitous. And Philip Knight, worth over $5 billion by the 1990s, was the epitome of the savvy businessman who knew how to steer his company through the shoals of the global marketplace.

But by the mid-1990s, this carefully woven strategy started to unravel for the Nikes of the world. The dirty little secrets of labor conditions in factories making shoes, clothing, and toys for brand-name companies began to hit the media. Kathie Lee Gifford was humiliated on prime-time television for using underpaid, underage Honduran girls to make her clothing line. Media reports cited Nike workers being hit with shoes, forced to work fourteen hour days, and as reported by Dara O'Rourke, one of the authors of the Ratcheting Labor Standards strategy described in this book, being poisoned by toxic glues. In the United States, seventy-two Thai workers were found locked in a Los Angeles sweatshop under slavelike conditions, producing clothing for brand-name U.S. companies.

Suddenly, the word "sweatshops," which had disappeared from the U.S. vernacular by the 1950s, was screeching across banner headlines, and groups in solidarity with factory workers sprang up throughout Europe and the United States. Religious groups disrupted shareholder meetings with anti-sweatshop resolutions. Campus groups staged sit-ins in their administrative offices demanding an end to the selling of "sweatshop products" in their campus stores. Soccer moms joined their high school daughters in noisy demonstrations outside retail stores. Comedians like late-night TV host Jay Leno mercilessly skewered brand-name companies in front of millions of Americans.

In a panic, companies realized that issuing press releases denying the sweatshop moniker was not enough. Something more had to be done, and quickly. That's where Codes of Conduct came in. With virtually no input from workers themselves, companies starting passing codes banning child labor and guaranteeing decent work conditions, and then beefing up their PR teams to go out and "sell" the codes to the public as a sign of their sincere commitment to social responsibility.

The companies battled with northern activist groups over the content of the codes, with activists pushing companies to include items like the internationally recognized rights of workers to freedom of association and collective bargaining, or a "living wage" instead of simply requiring that the factories comply with the local government's minimum wage. But the real battle was over how to ensure that the company's code was not just a lofty document on a piece of paper but something that had meaning on the ground.

Activists insisted that the codes be monitored by nonprofits that had a reputation for supporting workers' rights. Companies wanted accounting firms like Pricewaterhouse-Coopers that they felt more "comfortable" with, and began to hire them over the objections of many activists. The U.S. government promoted a mixed model with NGOs and accounting firms called the Fair Labor Association, and students came up with their own Worker Rights Consortium to investigate worker's complaints.

The U.S. unions, while supporting the students, were skeptical of the whole notion of codes and monitoring, which they saw as PR tools for companies or, even worse, efforts to replace the role of unions themselves. Instead of codes and monitors, the unions said, we should put our energies into helping workers form independent unions. The problem, however, is that in some countries, like China, such activity will land you in jail or a mental institution, and in other countries the government and businesses collude to keep unions weak or "company-friendly." When unions do get a real foothold, factory owners can just pick up stakes overnight and move to more business-friendly pastures. So while most activists and workers agree that strong, independent unions are ultimately the best way to enforce workers' rights, they also recognize that we are decades away from achieving that goal.

The alternative to the hodgepodge of codes and monitors would be national and international regulations that can be enforced with some kind of sanctioning power. But the only organization that sets labor standards, the International

Labor Organization, has no teeth when it comes to enforcement.

Fung, O'Rourke, and Sabel recognize the gaping hole between what is and what should be. To fill that gap, they have proposed a system for corporate disclosure of information that would inform the public about corporate labor and environmental standards and, they hope, pressure companies to "ratchet standards upward." While the commentators raise valid points about the feasibility of this scheme and the advisability of having a discredited organization like the World Bank oversee it, the proposal and the discussion it generates promises to lead us in the direction of a system where corporations would be truly accountable to workers, consumers, and the larger "stakeholder" community.

EDITORS' PREFACE

JOSHUA COHEN AND JOEL ROGERS

Hundreds of millions of people in the world work very hard, for very little, under hideous conditions. Most readers of this book benefit from that work—consider your shoes, or this morning's coffee. While most of us are unhappy about benefiting from the grinding toil of others, we are also unsure what to do about it.

Archon Fung, Dara O'Rourke, and Charles Sabel have a proposal, and it provides the focus for this New Democracy Forum on international labor standards. Their idea—"Ratcheting Labor Standards" (RLS)—is a strategy for improving wages and working conditions that is designed to be more sensitive to cross-national differences in economic development than a system of uniform standards with centralized enforcement, yet more demanding on companies than a voluntary scheme of corporate self-regulation. RLS builds on current efforts by international organizations to articulate labor standards; by social movements and unions to monitor the performance of companies and demand improvements; and by consumers to ensure that unethical companies do not succeed in the market. In the RLS framework, companies would be monitored by accounting firms, who would make full information about company practices available to unions, movements, and consumers; at the same time, practices in different economies would be compared to ensure that labor standards were as demanding as could reasonably be expected. If things work as planned, we get transparency plus constant pressure for improvement.

The respondents are unconvinced. Some argue that RLS is too demanding: high-wage enclaves might worsen surrounding misery, and pressures for constant improvement would make companies less willing to make initial reforms. Others worry that RLS is toothless: regulatory suppleness may mean vague standards that are too easily satisfied, and heavy reliance on markets and voluntary cooperation may mean insufficient attention to old-fashioned sanctions for bad behavior.

The troubling agreement among them all, however, is that this issue is of extraordinary moral magnitude, and that we are nearly clueless about how best to resolve it. It is hard to imagine an issue more worthy of our best thinking, and more in need of sharp debate.

1

REALIZING LABOR STANDARDS

Archon Fung, Dara O'Rourke, and Charles Sabel

This past fall, Nike was accused of using child labor in Cambodia. Not long before, Adidas was accused of using prison labor in China and sweatshop workers in El Salvador. Timberland, which trumpets its socially responsible business practices, was accused this year of employing 16-year-old girls in China, working them 98 hours per week, paying only 22 cents per hour, and all the while exposing them to toxic chemicals. New Balance has been criticized recently for anti-union practices and now produces the majority of its shoes in China, where independent unions are illegal.

Even "buying American" can mean paying for sweatshop labor. There are an estimated five thousand illegal, unregistered sweatshops in Los Angeles alone that label their products "Made in the USA." Only a few years ago, a company producing clothing for Mervyn's, Montgomery Ward, and BUM International, and selling their U.S.-labeled products on the racks of Macy's, Robinsons-May, and Filene's department stores, was found to employ Thai immigrant women who were working in virtual slave-labor conditions. And this company had recently passed a Department of Labor (DOL) inspection.

These conditions are repellent, and they have provoked a diffuse but insistent protest movement for international workers' rights. Resembling earlier social movements—for civil rights, women's equality, and environmental protection—the movement for workers' rights has already caught the attention of the public worldwide, and has provoked responses from multinational corporations, international organizations like the International Labor Organization (ILO) and the World Bank, and domestic regulatory authorities. And it has led to important but fragile cooperation between student groups, nongovernmental organizations (NGOs), and established trade unions.

Here, we propose a strategy for strengthening labor standards—norms that describe acceptable conditions of work and wages—that builds on, and connects, these disparate efforts. We call this approach "Ratcheting Labor Standards" (RLS). It charts a course beyond conventional top-down regulation based on uniform standards, and reliance on voluntary initiatives taken by corporations in response to social protest. A public debate has already emerged about how workplaces in the global economy should operate. The central aim of RLS is to create a transparent environment for that debate.

RLS would do two things. First, it would use monitoring and public disclosure of working conditions to create official, social, and financial incentives for firms to monitor and improve their own factories and those of their suppliers.

Second, it would create an easily accessible pool of information with which the best practices of leading firms could be publicly identified, compared, and diffused to others in comparable settings. We argue that the combination of firm-level incentives and an infrastructure for pooling results would help to set provisional minimum standards of corporate behavior, upon which competition—driven by social and regulatory pressures—would generate improvements that then "ratchet" standards upward.

Consider how RLS would work in the apparel industry. Firms operating in international markets, like Nike or the Gap, would be required to adopt a code of conduct and to participate in a social monitoring program. A firm would select a monitor from among NGOs or auditing companies that provide this service. The monitor would score the firms it regularly inspects according to their compliance with a code of conduct and their ability to correct violations. The monitor would report its findings to the firm and to the certifying agency to which the firm is a member.

The monitor would also report its findings to a "super monitor," an umpire constituted by international organizations such as the World Bank and the ILO, together with NGOs and international confederations of trade unions. This umpire organization would monitor the monitors, conduct inspections to verify their integrity, assure the comparability of monitoring data and methods, and make results accessible to the public.

By creating an umpire that opens social auditors and

firms to public scrutiny, this framework would extend and transform many current efforts to advance labor standards. Firms that depend on consumer loyalty would be eager to earn high grades. They would pressure less visible suppliers, and suppliers of suppliers, to follow suit. Activists, consumer groups, financial analysts, journalists, and many others would use RLS information to identify leaders and laggards in labor practices, press for improvements, establish norms of acceptable behavior, and pressure the monitors themselves to improve their auditing methods and to make their standards more demanding. Eventually NGOs, trade unions, or regulatory agencies might become monitors in this system. This would allow them to demonstrate the quality and reliability of the services they provide and to learn systematically from their peers.

Stepping back, the large purpose of RLS is to secure the most ambitious and feasible labor standards for workers *given their economic development context.* Standards emerge by comparing similarly situated facilities. The labor practices of a facility in Vietnam might be compared to one in Indonesia, but not initially to a European or North American facility. In this way, RLS encourages the incremental realization of demanding labor standards over time without imposing a uniform—and potentially protectionist—standard upon diverse contexts. By publicizing workplace conditions and practices, RLS enables society to sort out the abhorrent from the acceptable and shift its production methods from the former to the latter.

New Opportunities

Two recent developments in the organization of work account for many of the shortcomings of traditional strategies for dealing with the problem of labor standards, even as they create new regulatory opportunities: first, the increasing decentralization of production into tiered networks of *supply chains* that span the globe; second, the related recomposition of what is often called the *informal sector*.

It is no longer easy to determine where products as simple as baseball caps and sweatshirts or as complicated as computers and automobiles are made. That is because most name-brand manufacturers now market products that are co-designed and produced by networks of contractors and subcontractors. These networks obstruct accountability as much by their flux as by their intricacy. Manufacturers of products such as garments regularly switch countries, or even continents, as they switch suppliers. Far too many manufacturers hide behind these sprawling chains of ownership to deny responsibility for the factories that produce their goods.

But even as regulators lose oversight, corporations have markedly increased their ability to monitor suppliers. Relations between customers and suppliers were traditionally arms-length attachments made and broken solely on the basis of prices, which were often just a reflection of wage levels. Under contemporary globalization, these relationships are increasingly based on careful and continuous assessments of firms as potential partners who must provide not only cheap labor, but also product and process improvements that increase competitiveness for the whole production chain. The most sophisticated firms manage their supply chains by ranking suppliers according to their capacities as co-developers and their ability to meet quality, logistical, and diversity goals. Suppliers must show increasing capabilities to maintain and increase their status in these hierarchies.

Now focused on increasing profit and product quality, these supply-chain practices can potentially be used to improve labor standards. In contemporary footwear production, for example, the largest supplier is a Taiwanese firm called Pou Chen. This conglomerate produces for, among others, Nike, Reebok, Adidas, Fila, Puma, and Timberland. Because of consumer awareness and advocacy pressures, the brands now work closely with Pou Chen to improve labor conditions in their factories. They send their own internal compliance staff to evaluate Pou Chen facilities and hire external auditors to measure whether Pou Chen is meeting their codes of conduct. Some brands then rank these suppliers—including Pou Chen's competitors—by measures that reflect labor and environmental conditions. Though incorporating social considerations into contemporary supplier management strategies is still rare, a central goal of RLS is to make it more widespread.

* * *

The second important development is the persistence, and often the expansion, of the informal sector: women piece-workers stitching baseball covers in their homes, street vendors selling piece goods on behalf of large distributors, skilled artisans working wood, stone, metal, or plastic with simple machines, brickmakers supplying small construction sites. Although exact numbers are hard to come by, evidence suggests that informal-sector workers in general, and women workers who are based at home in particular, account for a significant share of employment in export industries in developing countries.[1]

Transformations of global supply chains have also recast these activities in ways that both obstruct familiar forms of accountability and open the way to new ones. Competition from world-class firms and from the import of secondhand products from richer economies can push weak domestic producers into the informal sector and increase competition there. This undoes the unwritten rules of the informal sector—the social conventions and practices framing wages, business relationships, and working conditions—diminishing whatever social accountability there was.

But improbable as it seems at first glance, this effect may be partially offset by changes connected to new supplier relations. The same logistical and quality standards that govern global production generally govern subcontracting from the formal sector to the informal sector today. Customers in the formal sector usually use their superior bargaining power to make informal-sector producers pay the costs of failing to meet quality and timeliness requirements.

But the most ambitious and capable among the informal producers see that they can get ahead by mastering the same disciplines of process control, monitoring, and innovation that yield such large returns for their partners in the formal sector. Already, operators in the informal sector are becoming familiar with relevant technical protocols, just as many of them gained expertise in secondhand machinery long ago.

The distance between the formal and informal sectors is thus not as great as it at first appears. Many informal producers are not only connected to global production chains through their goods, but also potentially through organizational practices that bridge the formal/informal divide. These connections may allow the most able informal firms to cross that gap in time. Those that do may be subject to regulatory mechanisms that are emerging in the formal sector.

New Ways to Regulate

Labor and environmental regulators have noted these structural changes and have developed programs that take into account the organization of modern supply chains, the vulnerabilities for firms that result from them, and new forms of public pressure generated in part by the new regulatory regime.

One example that underscores the growing importance of supply-chain dependencies is the Labor Department's decade-old "No Sweat" program, which has raised labor standards compliance in the garment sectors of New York, San Francisco, and Los Angeles.[2] Much of the work of cutting, sewing, and packaging clothing is done by immigrants in sweatshops employing one to two dozen workers. Thousands of fly-by-night operations have long scoffed at inspections, sanctions, and other familiar methods to ensure compliance.

But when retailers and manufacturers adopted "lean retailing" and "just-in-time" production techniques to lower costs, reduce cycle times, and shrink inventories, they also opened themselves to clever regulators in two ways. First, regulators could stop business along the entire supply chain by stopping it at any one point. The obscure "hot cargo" provision of the 1938 Fair Labor Standards Act gave them the power to do just this. This provision makes it unlawful for any person "to transport, offer for transportation, ship, deliver, or sell in commerce . . . any goods in the production of which any employee was employed in violation" of the Act.

Second, because "lean retailing" methods increase communication and control between firms, regulators could use this leverage to make large firms responsible for the behavior of their smaller suppliers. So, when regulators catch small firms in violation of labor law, they now often use their power of delay to compel retailers and large manufacturers to sign "Compliance Monitoring Agreements," under which firms agree to monitor, usually through third-party social-auditing firms, the compliance of their small supplier shops. By 1999, nearly half of contractor shops in New York, San Francisco, and Los Angeles were covered by such agreements, and shops covered by such agreements tend to comply with wage and hours regulations more often than those that are not.

Three innovations in environmental regulation offer further lessons for labor regulators.

The Massachusetts Toxics Use Reduction Act (TURA) builds on capabilities for self-monitoring and continuous improvement that firms must regularly acquire in order to compete. The act requires hundreds of firms that produce or release certain amounts of listed toxics to develop "Toxics Use Reduction Plans." In preparing these plans, engineers, managers, and workers typically work in teams to review possible ways to reduce the plant's reliance on toxic inputs, its generation of toxic by-products, and the danger of toxic releases to the environment. Studies suggest that this mobilization of local knowledge and expertise generates far more effective pollution prevention and toxics reductions than regulators would have thought feasible. Indeed, many plans yield not only environmental improvements but also financial savings; though firms are not required to implement their plans, many do so because of the compelling advantages that legally imposed self-examination reveals.[3]

A related Massachusetts program called "Environmental Results" also encourages firms to develop their own compliance and improvement strategies, but aims at thousands of dry cleaners, printers, photo developers, and auto-body operations. What makes the program relevant here is that, for regulators, these small enterprises are equivalent to operations in the informal sector: government agencies are often unaware of their existence and lack the resources to inspect them. Instead of traditional inspection, regulators pursue outreach and capacity-building. Working through industry associations to locate and contact these small businesses, regulators provide each firm with workbooks detailing the steps necessary to reach environmental compliance. Firms are then required to certify to regulators that they have followed these steps. Evaluators estimate that this program has increased the number of firms known to regulators fivefold, and that it has accomplished substantial reductions in the emissions of hazardous and smog-producing air pollutants.[4]

Other related environmental strategies produce information that allows the public to make well-targeted demands for corporate reform. Perhaps the oldest and best known is the U.S. Toxics Release Inventory (TRI). Begun in 1988, the TRI requires some 23,000 facilities to report annually their releases of some 650 chemicals to a publicly accessible database. This information is used by ordinary citizens, activists, journalists, and managers, among others, to identify firms that pollute heavily. These "dirty" companies often become the subject of bad publicity, punishment in financial markets, and direct citizen action.[5] Firms both respond and pre-empt these critics by reducing their use and release of TRI chemicals. Though causation is difficult to assign, some evidence shows that TRI has contributed to some of the 1.5 billion pound (that is, 45 percent) reduction in releases of listed chemicals between 1988 and 1998.[6] Though the TRI is the largest of these "information-based" disclosure efforts, programs that rely on publicity, information, and citizen response have also been initiated in Western Europe, Indonesia, the Philippines, and other countries.[7]

The "No Sweat" regulatory program depends on the threat of severe penalties—a threat that is now more credible because of the high costs of supply-chain disruption. But TRI, TURA, and "Environmental Results" (via the participation of publicity-sensitive trade associations) depend on the concern of citizens for their environment. Is there similar public concern for the welfare of (often distant) workers?

Ethical Consumerism

The most direct evidence of public concern about harsh labor conditions comes from surveys of consumer preferences and willingness to pay premiums based on the social and ethical character of firms and their production processes. In 1999, Marymount University's Center for Ethical Concerns conducted a telephone survey of U.S. consumer attitudes about garment production.[8] Three-quarters of the respondents reported that they would avoid shopping at a retailer whom they knew to sell garments made in sweatshops. Eighty-six percent report that they would pay an extra dollar on a twenty-dollar garment if they could be sure that it was made under non-sweated conditions. Similarly, a survey conducted in 1998 found that "80 percent of respondents said that they would not buy products made under poor conditions or that they were willing to pay more if they knew the items were made under good conditions."[9]

Environics International conducted a massive study of international opinion on these questions in 1999. The survey asked 25,000 individuals in 23 countries for their attitudes about corporate social responsibility. Though respondents from North America and Western Europe felt more strongly than those from developing nations, large minorities everywhere felt that major companies had responsibilities as ethical and social leaders. In North America, 51 percent of respondents reported punishing a company for being socially irresponsible in the past year, while 39 percent of Northern European respondents claimed to have done so.[10]

The emergence of ethical consumerism includes not only labor and product concerns, but also investment choices. Over the past decade, socially responsible investing has grown dramatically and far outpaced the expansion of investment generally. Between 1995 and 1999, the total assets in mutual funds utilizing "social screens" that exclude firms that produce tobacco, manufacture firearms, or degrade the environment grew almost tenfold, from $162 billion to $1.5 *trillion.* At the end of 1999, one out of every eight dollars under professional management in the United States was part of a portfolio claiming to be socially responsible.[11]

Corporations and NGOs

Skeptics may doubt that survey responses translate into choices at the shopping mall, but high-profile multinational corporations take the polling data seriously. Prodded by the opinions it reveals, as well as by activist campaigns, boycotts, campus protests, and media exposés, companies like Nike, the Gap, and Levi's act as though they assume consumers care about social conditions and consequences of production processes. Labor and environmental considerations have been added to the long list of dimensions on which they compete for a share of the market.[12]

Some of these firms have responded directly to public pressure by incorporating labor and other social priorities into the protocols by which they manage production in their supply chains. All of the main garment, shoe, and toy companies—Nike, Reebok, Adidas, Levi's, Disney, Mattel, the Gap—now have programs in place that combine codes of conduct, in-house assessment, and assistance from third parties to monitor supplier compliance with these codes.

The public, however, is skeptical about the sincerity and

effectiveness of these efforts, and given the continuing scandals, rightfully so. This skepticism has led to the proliferation of independent monitoring and third-party social certification programs in the United States and Europe. Consulting and financial auditing firms such as Ernst & Young, PricewaterhouseCoopers (PwC), SGS International Certification Services, Cal Safety Compliance Corporation, Bureau Veritas Quality International, and Det Norske Veritas have recognized this growing market and begun to offer themselves as social inspectors. PwC and Cal Safety conducted over six thousand and ten thousand social audits last year, respectively.

But skepticism and critiques of the audits performed by these firms—audits paid for, after all, by client companies—has led to the establishment of third-party systems for evaluating and certifying monitors and for systematically comparing factory performance.[13] A growing number of NGOs compete in this certification market. For example, the Fair Labor Association (FLA), convened by the Clinton administration in 1996, is the most advanced but quite controversial. The FLA will certify its first external auditors in early 2001 and hopes to begin the auditing which will lead to certifying sweat-free brands by the end of the year. SA8000, created in 1997 by the Council on Economic Priorities (CEP), is patterned on the ISO family of standards and requires corporations to hire certified auditors to evaluate the conduct of individual factories. The Clean Clothes Campaign, made up of a coalition of activists across

Europe, plans to establish a foundation that will certify monitors, collect funds from member firms, and then pay monitoring organizations directly. The Worker Rights Consortium (WRC), developed by the United Students Against Sweatshops (USAS) in 1999, focuses on forcing out information, creating verification systems, and being proactive about inspections. The WRC differs from the other models in that it will explicitly not certify company compliance with a code of conduct or standard.

The Next Step

Regulatory innovations, corporate initiatives in reaction to ethical consumerism, and the spread of third-party audits and certification programs create building blocks for a coherent response to international labor abuses, but don't yet constitute one. The regulatory innovations have not crystallized into a robust, comprehensive system in the environmental area. In their present form they scarcely constitute a direct model for labor regulation. Consumer activism and corporate responses to it are still too narrowly focused on brand-sensitive firms. And, even putting to one side the problem of limited scope, the proliferation of certification bodies and monitoring businesses means there is no common metric by which to credibly compare companies. Without such a level playing field, firms can't demonstrate the sincerity or the effectiveness of their workplace efforts to workers or consumers. And even the best of these programs still lack much information about the most effective means to implement real improvements for workers after problems are identified.

Ratcheting Labor Standards addresses these obstacles systematically.

Principles

Four principles—transparency, competitive comparison, continuous improvement, and sanctions—can guide activists, consumers, public officials, and managers in building an encompassing framework to organize these efforts.

The principle of *transparency* suggests a world in which consumers, workers, activists, and the public at large have the information they need to accurately and confidently identify initiatives to improve labor standards, gauge the results of those efforts, and compare the successes of firms, localities, and even nations against one another.

There are many opponents and few champions of transparency in labor standards. No firm wants to be the first to open itself to public scrutiny. Those who have unilaterally exposed themselves to public examination often have been punished, and their experience makes them, and others, reluctant to continue. In May 1998, for example, Reebok joined with an Indonesian organization called Insan Hitawasana Sejahtera (IHS) to improve working conditions in two factories producing Reebok athletic wear in Indonesia. Following the plan of the project, called Peduli Hak ("Caring for Rights"), the group released a report detailing short-comings in factory operations, such as minimum-wage violations, illegal overtime, hazardous chemicals and machinery, and poor ventilation and lighting. Factory managers took steps to address nearly all of the issues identified in the report. They invested over $500,000, and achieved substantial improvements in many areas.

To the dismay of Reebok executives and IHS, however, activists and journalists used the report as an exposé opportunity to publicize the violations at these facilities. Without the ability to compare the condition of these factories to those of its competitors, Reebok and IHS suffered severe public rebuke rather than the kudos they may have deserved.

And even in the absence of such perverse incentives, impulses to secrecy make companies reluctant to disclose even the most basic details of their operations. Private and non-profit social-auditing firms often consider their methods and results to be sources of competitive advantage and proprietary knowledge. Transparency also ranks low on the agendas of many activists, who typically marshal their resources to secure more immediately tangible programs or codes of conduct from corporations.

Against these obstacles, some activists have recently begun to demand that multinational producers disclose the locations of their production facilities and those of their suppliers. Even such basic information can help establish whether companies are complying with their stated codes of conduct, and can lay the groundwork for documenting conditions in their facilities. Firms initially balked, and complained that such disclosure would jeopardize crucial trade secrets. But several large producers, responding to pressure from student groups, have agreed to disclose the locations of suppliers that produce goods that are branded with university names.[14] Nike has raised the bar for transparency, perhaps easing the path for others to follow, by releasing internal social-auditing information. Its reports included the number and type of violations (wages, child labor, health, and safety) of its internal code found at some of its seven hundred factories, and the action plans of these factories to address the violations.[15] The company calls this program "Transparency 101."

These developments hint at a vision of full social transparency. One of its mechanisms might be databases that collect social performance metrics such as facility locations, wage levels, workforce age profiles, health and safety conditions, environmental impacts of multinational producers, and their long supply chains. Beyond actual social performance, however, full transparency also demands that firms disclose their methods for monitoring social performance and procedures for improving workplace conditions and eliminating legal and code of conduct violations.

Full transparency would make possible the second principle of RLS: *competitive comparison.* High-profile companies currently compete informally to protect and build their reputations as socially responsible actors. When Nike responded to critics by disclosing the locations of 44 facilities producing goods for universities on its website, five of its competitors—Jansport, GEAR for Sports, Champion, EastPak, and Russell—quickly followed suit. But detailed information (for example, who works in those factories, their working conditions, their pay, and their hours) is not yet available.

More complete and transparent performance data of this sort would enable governments, pressure groups, publics, the media, and companies themselves to make precise and quick assessments of labor conditions of firms in comparison to their competitors. It would expand the scope of companies currently vying for consumer loyalty on social grounds, because those who refused to socially compare themselves would be presumed to be very poor performers. Transparency would create an even playing field for this competition, and firms like Reebok would be rewarded, instead of punished, for bold innovations like its Peduli Hak initiative.

The third principle of RLS is *continuous improvement* in both firm social performance and labor standards. This grows out of the principle of competitive comparison. Social and market pressures would push firms—perhaps working with public agencies, NGOs, or unions—to constantly develop new methods of improving occupational health and safety, labor management practices, and the like.

Nike's recent series of labor initiatives, each of which was superior to its predecessor, illustrates how social and competitive pressure can generate continuous improvement in labor performance. Responding to early protests and a number of exposés regarding its treatment of workers in countries like Indonesia, Nike adopted a code of conduct for itself and its manufacturers in 1992. In response to complaints that these codes were without force, the company hired Ernst and Young, among others, to conduct external audits of its suppliers' compliance with the code. After critics revealed serious omissions and errors in these reports, Nike responded by incorporating social priorities into its regular supplier management practices, in programs called SHAPE (Safety, Health, Attitude, People, and Environment) and MESH (Management, Environment, Safety, Health), which were modeled on ISO 14000 and other labor management principles. Under continuing activist scrutiny and pressure, Nike eventually settled on hiring PricewaterhouseCoopers to monitor labor and environmental conditions in all of its factories worldwide. These monitoring programs, while still coming under criticism, have resulted in reductions of orders and cancellation of contracts from facilities with serious social violations. Even more recently, the corporation has embarked on several partnerships with local nongovernmental organizations and launched its "Transparency 101" program.

Knowledgeable critics contend that these efforts are not enough. Still, the company's steps do indicate serious responses. More importantly, some of these measures empower observers to assess the veracity of its claims and actual progress. Nike has perhaps been on the hot seat with regard to labor standards longer than any other multinational corporation, and its painstaking initiatives result in large measure from this pressure. RLS aims to spread this attention and compulsion to many more firms, and thus broadly engender the dynamic of continuous improvement in workplace conditions.

If this were done, the norms of acceptable social performance, or labor standards, could emerge from evolving practices. As firms improve, the standards should regularly become more demanding. This dynamic encourages producers to seek novel ways to improve their labor conditions and outcomes and publicly explain how they are doing so. It would be a race to the top in which firms sought to outdo one another in social performance, just as they now compete on more conventional dimensions. We constantly demand better quality and prices from the products that firms produce. Why should we settle for fixed, minimum standards in workplace conditions, rather than demanding that those improve as quickly as economic and technological conditions permit?

The final principle of RLS involves *sanctions*. Many of the developments that inform this approach—such as protest and consumer response, social accreditation and auditing schemes, and ethical consumerism—occur voluntarily through civic action and corporate response. More forceful regulatory institutions backed by punishments, however, are necessary to extend and deepen the promising dynamics behind these trends. The full system of transparency, competitive comparison, and continuous improvement requires both formal and informal sanctions. Since the RLS approach offers distinctive methods for setting standards and achieving compliance, its basis of sanctions also differs from conventional regulation, where firms are punished for failing to meet minimum performance criteria. Again, we must look for alternatives to traditional sanctions (which punish firms for failing to meet established standards) because these can encourage firms to evade the monitoring and comparison that is essential to improving labor conditions.

Instead, RLS would use public power to dislodge information that would in turn trigger more nuanced and ultimately powerful incentives to improve social performance. Sanctions should, therefore, be applied in a way that advances the prior principles of transparency and continuous improvement. On the former, firms that fail to disclose their labor outcomes or monitoring methods should be presumed to have something to hide, and be punished for violating the first norm. On the latter, truly recalcitrant firms, deserving of the harshest castigation that the regime can offer, are those whom comparison identifies as laggards in labor performance and who fail to adopt measures that have proven effective for their peers.

Practice

From the top, RLS would be governed by a council that perhaps emerges from one of the current nongovernmental social-certification organizations or from a collaboration between intergovernmental organizations. That governing umpire would regulate two kind of entities: firms and monitors.

Firms in an RLS regulated sector, say footwear or textiles, would each select a monitoring entity and abide by its particular protocols. In RLS, monitors are organizations that collect and verify social-performance information and help firms comply with their labor standards. Private social-auditing concerns, the internal labor compliance staff of multinationals, and public regulatory agencies such as state and national departments of labor, each currently perform these functions. Firms would be required to report wages, workforce profiles, environmental and labor management systems, and similar elements of social performance to their monitor. They would also submit to the latter's inspection and verification protocols and social-management procedures. RLS would also require firms to periodically open themselves to independent audits from NGOs, governmental bodies, or even unions to prevent collusion and assure veracity of reported data.

These monitors would then rank the social performance of firms under their purview. Monitors would be required to report these rankings, the methods used to derive and verify them, and basic social performance data of firms to the governing body. This umpire would assure the comparability of the information on key dimensions and disseminate much of it publicly.

These arrangements would create a two-sided, mutually reinforcing competition between firms and monitors. Firms that are confident of their outstanding social performance would seek out the most credible monitoring organizations to verify their accomplishments. The best monitors would seek outstanding social performers in order to hone their evaluative skills, build their reputations, and expand their influence. In the first instance, this process would establish a competition of sorts in workplace conditions and labor performance among the regulated entities. Firms would vie to show consumers and regulators that they are better than their competitors.

In the medium term, the RLS framework would generate a vast amount of information that does not currently exist about how firms actually perform socially and about how to improve that performance. This knowledge could be used by an array of actors and generate complementary competitive pressures on firms. Hundreds of millions of socially sensitive consumers would utilize these data in their purchasing decisions. Journalists, activists, and investors would use the information to shame poorly performing companies. They would also use it to expose poor monitors and demand increased veracity. Responsible firms could assume that their behavior would be rewarded and irresponsible firms would fear embarrassment, pressure campaigns, official sanctions, and, worst of all, loss of market share. Firms themselves would therefore use this knowledge to benchmark their performance and to learn how they might improve it.

Perhaps most importantly, this knowledge would inform a wide-ranging, inclusive, and often heated public debate on global labor conditions. Participants in this debate would argue for particular standards and improvements—with respect to child labor or workplace health, for example—by referring to the successful, and therefore feasible, efforts in various contexts. Pushed by this public debate, officials at local, national, or international levels could use information generated by RLS to formulate minimum substantive labor standards based on actual performance and procedural standards for improvement. They might also use the data, as some regulators now use TRI environmental information, to better enforce existing regulations.

It is crucial that the voices of workers in developing countries be present in this debate. Though international labor standards are pursued in their name, they are too seldom heard in discussions about standards and enforcement. RLS offers a way to connect the knowledge and preferences of workers to the power of well-intentioned consumers and activists in wealthy nations. RLS aims to enhance the conditions of workplaces without the protectionist effects that can come from uniform standards. RLS derives its labor standards from the best practices of workplaces under similar economic circumstances. These standards are demanding because they are based on what the leaders have done, yet demonstrably feasible because they have been implemented under competitive and comparable conditions. The goal of these demanding and feasible labor standards is to make workplaces in developing countries as good as they can be without imposing requirements that drive investment and employment away. Striking that delicate balance will require the knowledge, and ultimately the judgment, of the workers in these facilities.

That balance, moreover, will change over time as firms and workers enhance their social performance possibilities. RLS standards would therefore be periodically revised—ratcheted upward—to reflect these changes. Unlike conventional regulation, these corrigible yet enforceable standards would be the product—not the starting point—of a process that was centrally focused on producing widely accessible and accurate knowledge of actual practices and deploying that knowledge to improve practices over time.

Getting There

RLS principles are now expressed in a limited set of cases, such as Nike and other high-profile firms. How might they become a wider regulatory framework? We can envision at least two roads to begin building RLS.

On the first, one of the existing nongovernmental, multi-stakeholder workplace monitoring initiatives—such as the Clean Clothes Campaign, FLA, Workers Rights Consortium, or SA8000—could embrace RLS as an expansion strategy. These programs currently compete with one another. One entity, however, could differentiate itself from the others through a focus on transparency and disclosure that breaks with now-dominant policies of confidentiality and proprietary knowledge. This innovation, while scaring off some corporations fearful of revealing current practices, would make this organization the most credible, encompassing, and capable social-certification entity. This credibility would allow it to impose significant disclosure requirements on its associated firms and monitors, to rank each of them on their social performance, and to set the terms of open comparison for other firms and monitors. The WRC may be closest to moving in this direction, as its university members are least likely to oppose broad public transparency and comparison.

Alternatively, transnational organizations such as the ILO, the United Nations, or the World Bank could begin to build RLS. All three claim to be moved by sincere concern for the impact of globalization on labor, the environment, women, and native peoples. In addition, the World Bank, given its dedication to free trade and free markets, may see RLS as a lesser evil compared to the imposition of trade clauses. Since world public opinion demands some response to scandalous labor conditions, the Bank may prefer a system based on transparency, in which firms play an important role in determining operational details, to regulation imposed by distant central authorities.

One or several of these international bodies might begin by establishing an umbrella stakeholder group, composed perhaps of corporate, national, NGO, labor, and monitoring firms, to begin a formal process of building RLS. This body would set minimum performance and procedural standards for firms. It would also require them to report on their own monitoring protocols and results, and then publicly disclose this information. This organization could be a precursor or sponsor to the super monitor, or umpire-governance body. A key first step in this process would be to call together the existing monitors and certification bodies for an initial "transparency event" in order to discuss the ground rules, objectives, demonstration cases, and first steps to establishing RLS regulation.

By now, even sympathetic readers may suspect that we advance by wishful thinking and assume key actors share our perspectives and goals, when even casual inspection of the newspapers suggests they do not. More bluntly, many will suspect, and others firmly believe, that the World Bank, like the International Monetary Fund (IMF), prefers a deregulated world, one in which labor is disciplined by the market and firms by each other. And if the ILO is a promising partner, why are NGOs so prominent in new movements that the ILO, given its mandate and history, should be leading? There are other reasons one might be doubtful. What about national trade unions and regulatory authorities, the traditional backbone of labor protection in the developed economies? Are they meant to stand idly by as the rest of the world ratchets itself into a new regulatory regime? If not, what part might they play in shaping new strategies and institutions? In short, haven't we been far too hasty in jumping from economic and social trends to institutional answers, assuming in the optimistic rush that major actors will automatically shift to new roles in RLS?

In response to these doubts, we argue that the World Bank could become an important collaborator in the new system. Many will question whether institutions like the Bank could, or would, become an ally for forceful labor standards, but we argue that it is already being transformed in ways that could belie its reputation as an enemy of regulation. Space permitting, a case for the ILO's cooperation could also be made. We also argue that national regulators and trade unions, whose opposition could block RLS, might come to see this initiative as an opportunity to advance their own internal reforms.

The World Bank

The transformation of the World Bank grows directly out of its current, discrete, crisis. The Bank's role in its traditional business of financing major infrastructure projects such as dams and roads in developing countries is being eclipsed. For one thing, as demand for such project finance has grown, private lenders have entered this market, providing funds at affordable rates without the red tape that encumbers Bank transactions. For another, the Bank's recurrent public pummeling for the adverse environmental and social consequences of its largest investment projects have reduced the areas in which it is able to operate.

Without a clear mission in financial stabilization or infrastructure development, the Bank is left with "softer" tasks, which are captured in its new self-characterization as "the knowledge Bank": fighting official corruption, fomenting the rule of law, improving environmental protection, encouraging entrepreneurship, and redesigning social protection systems. All of these, however, require the same starting points as RLS: increased transparency, heightened accountability, and decentralized learning through the local adaptation of best practices. Unsurprisingly, therefore, many ground-level Bank officials who participate in these project areas already have experience using best practices to fix local goals and building problem-solving coalitions to achieve them. This new breed of Bank staffers often bring NGOs and official institutions together to define goals and assess progress. Indeed, they often use shifting alliances of this kind against entrenched interests, such as corrupt government agencies. For this group within the Bank, RLS could help to authorize and formalize their own methods and strategies.

But RLS also appeals to higher-ups at the Bank for reasons of convenience. Powerful governments with representatives on the Bank's board of directors, such as the United States, have in recent years pressured the Bank to deny loans to countries that violate the ILO's core standards. Bank officials demur at the prospect of becoming an enforcement agency for the ILO, and some embrace RLS as a possible counterproposal. In emphasizing competition as a means of stopping bad practices and diffusing better ones, RLS sounds a familiar chord in the Bank: the new "knowledge Bank" professes to be even more "market driven" than its predecessor.

The appeal is not just tactical and terminological. At least some officials in the Bank see the kind of integrative knowledge-pooling used to build the "soft infrastructure" of working schools, reliable health care, and clean government as a kind of re-regulation. In this light, RLS is compatible with, and perhaps in some sense a model for, an emergent regulatory regime. Exploration of RLS can play a small part in the re-orientation of Bank strategy. It can, moreover, play a related operational role: pressed by human rights advocates and local NGOs, the Bank has already adopted policies requiring it to consider the impacts of its activities on the environment, on indigenous peoples, and on the condition of women.

It does not follow from all this that the Bank is a partisan for RLS. But neither is it an adversary with inimical interests. There is no more and no less than a real possibility that the Bank could link internal reorientation to institutional participation in the creation of a new kind of labor standard along the lines of RLS.

Unions and Regulators

Consider, finally, the potential effects of RLS on trade unions and regulatory authorities. These organizations are struggling against a marginalization that calls into question their traditional roles and effectiveness. Some labor leaders and regulators may fear RLS as yet another wave in the tides of deregulation and economic transformation. They may identify it as part of the family of privatized, self-regulation initiatives that chip away at public regulation. Such initiatives seem to strive for standards without regulators, in which corporations monitor and improve themselves on their own terms. Critics charge with good reason that such programs offer scant social protection.

But, as we have tried to make clear, RLS aims not to deregulate, but rather to re-deploy public power in ways that extend its regulatory reach and wisdom. Those who misread the proposal as a concession to unfettered markets will also miss many novel ways in which RLS can strengthen the hands and extend the horizons of those who have long championed workplace improvements.

Officials in national and local regulatory agencies, for example, could use information in RLS to bolster their own enforcement activities by identifying local violators, just as some environmental agencies now use TRI. A more ambitious step would be legislation requiring domestic firms to participate in RLS. This would shift much of the burden of inspection and compliance monitoring from national regulators to the international regime, allowing the former to concentrate on the worst performers. States could use the performance standards and benchmarks that emerge from RLS to adjust their own official labor standards or to create a differentiated set of "performance tracks." At the end of this harmonization trajectory, states could transform their own regulatory systems from fixed-rule to ratcheting by requiring domestic firms to score high on RLS measures or face sanctions. Along the way, regulatory agencies could join RLS as certified monitors. This would compel them to compete with and learn from similarly certified regulators in other countries, private sector innovators, and capable NGOs. A similar logic applies to unions. At the least, unions participating in RLS could gain otherwise unobtainable information about intricate supply chains. Unions could use RLS-generated information to learn about best and worst practices in an industry, and they could use this data to inform and strengthen their position during collective bargaining. RLS rankings of particular corporations would also allow them to identify the worst performers and target them through corporate campaigns, boycotts, or shareholder actions.

As a further step, unions might themselves become certified monitors. Many labor leaders claim that the best monitors of any workplace are the workers themselves, and RLS allows them to make this claim credible. As RLS is an open system that encourages participation from all fronts, trade unions would certainly be a welcome source of monitoring expertise. The best union monitors could use RLS rankings to show that they were superior to private-sector, non-worker competitors. By showing credible third parties that they monitor better than others—because, for example, they have better access to information from workers on real factory conditions and have the expertise to propose remedies to the problems they uncover—they would be renewing the public's trust in their claim that they are the most capable advocates of worker interests. By ranking monitors and acting as certified monitors themselves, unions that participate in RLS would dramatically expand their knowledge of workplace problems and how to fix them. In time, they would renew and improve the services they provide and thereby reclaim the loyalty of current members and attract new ones as well.

Since workers must form coherent organizations to conduct social audits and workplace monitoring, freedom of association is an essential implication of RLS. Unions could therefore also use RLS to press governments and corporations to respect the freedoms that workers require to collectively understand and improve their workplaces. Just as its market-like characteristics of competition and transparency should generate support from corporations and the

World Bank, RLS's democratic stress on inclusiveness, participation, and association should resonate with trade unions and NGOs.

A Global Problem

Even as contemporary globalization makes us complicit in terrible abuses of workers, it opens up new possibilities for public action to mitigate these wrongs. These possibilities come from the increasing capabilities of corporations—under the pressure of public revulsion at their social practices—to improve workplace conditions through the same sophisticated management strategies that make them champions of the current globalization in first place.

We have argued that the best way to exploit these possibilities is through a new kind of labor regulation—Ratcheting Labor Standards—that relies on information, competition, and the participation of not only regulators and firms but also workers, consumers, journalists, investors, NGOs, and the public at large. RLS promises labor standards that are feasible because they are based on actual best practices, and non-protectionist because they take into account differences in contexts of economic development. These labor standards, moreover, join the limited enforcement power of government to the potentially great disciplinary forces of social pressure and market competition. They aim, finally, not at establishing a minimum fixed set of core workplace rights, but rather at creating a process that makes workplaces as good as they can be, and better over time, as companies become more capable and nations more developed.

Our proposal for RLS, like the regulatory project it is meant to advance, raises at least as many questions as it answers. Is the approach only appropriate for multinational companies who sell to consumers in rich countries? Or can it also apply to commodity producers or those who sell primarily to domestic markets in developing countries? We believe that labor under the latter conditions will benefit from the general RLS approach to regulation, but the institutions and programs will obviously differ. Does RLS improbably require the majority of consumers to be sensitive to labor issues? Or, can relatively few attentive consumers and activists combine with media exposure, investor concerns, and public grading to leverage changes in the behavior and priorities of corporations? We believe that reputation is so critical today, and improving labor standards so feasible, that a public ranking system like RLS would amplify even relatively few voices into substantial workplace improvements. Already, the tiny fraction of customers of Nike, Reebok, and Mattel who have expressed concerns on labor issues have induced substantial shifts in corporate policy. But will RLS indeed make this increase in the scope of reform self-reinforcing?

The best way to answer these and other crucial questions, we think, is to engage in discussion with a view toward actually constructing the system. Given how many building blocks of RLS are already in place, and also how many possibilities for critical review would be afforded by even a flawed version of the system, the best way to test and improve RLS is to create the transparency and comparability of monitoring on which the full-fledged regime depends. Sometimes looking while leaping can be prudent.

Earnest engagement in such discussion will not be easy for many, as elements of RLS are strange and potentially threatening. Many corporate actors want an even playing field on which to establish their credibility as ethical actors, yet fear public scrutiny and transparency. For many NGOs and unions, "competition" smacks of privatization and market violence, and collaboration with firms to raise labor standards smells of co-optation. Yet some activists, impatient for progress, have pioneered impressive cooperative workplace monitoring and improvement projects with willing multinationals. Many official regulators are loathe to endorse a regulatory approach that depends upon so many forms of public participation and creates intimate connections to the private sector. Still, these same regulators recognize the limits of their conventional strategies in the current economic environment and are searching for more effective methods.

Our hope in this essay is to offer a labor standards strategy that allows us all to re-examine and test our programmatic commitments without sacrificing the possibilities of concerted action. How else can we hope to find effective solutions to the new misery of the global economy?

2

A BETTER MOUSETRAP?

ROBIN BROAD

Archon Fung, Dara O'Rourke, and Charles Sabel are to be commended for devising their creative "Ratcheting Labor Standards" (RLS), for attempting to add details and teeth to monitoring plans, for their focus on public disclosure, and for their thoughtful discussion of informal versus formal sectors and domestic versus export sectors. This is exactly the sort of new proposal that deserves broad discussion and might advance the work against corporate-led globalization. Without such concrete proposals we are unlikely to move beyond the current wave of scattered corporate codes of conduct, which are still in their early stages of experimentation.

We also need more such proposals on the table because we (individuals and groups, activists and scholars, North and South) need to learn how to discuss the advantages and disadvantages of any given proposal without turning disagreements into divisive debates. To be blunt, much of the debate about codes of conduct over the last few years has involved bickering among should-be allies. Case in point is the debate between proponents of the Fair Labor Association and the Workers' Rights Consortium, which involves a dispute over the merits of two plans, neither of which has been tested broadly in the field.

Let me take up the authors' call to engage in discussion about their proposal and share five questions that RLS raises for me. I pose these as food-for-thought—and not criticisms—to the authors and to other academics and activists working on proposals to make trade and investment more socially and environmentally responsible.

1. RIGHTS OR STANDARDS?

Fung, O'Rourke, and Sabel propose using labor standards of varying stringencies to "secure the most ambitious feasible labor standards for workers given their economic development context . . . without imposing a uniform, and potentially protectionist, standard upon diverse contexts." My own view is that the only way to avoid charges of protectionism is not to rely exclusively on diverse and flexible standards but to have uniform rights that should be recognized whatever the context. In the 1980s, groups such as the International Labor Rights Fund sought to specify the relevant rights: they studied seventy years of International Labor Organization (ILO) deliberations during which employees, worker representatives, and governments negotiated over one hundred international conventions on labor. From these conventions, the Fund culled a list of six internationally agreed-upon core worker rights, including freedom of association and the right to collective bargaining. Using these basic labor rights avoids a major pitfall: having to determine which standards are appropriate for which corporations or which levels of development—a potentially messy judgment call.

2. Northern-Based Codes of Conduct versus Grassroots Union Activism?

The other benefit of using core rights is that it clearly delineates a role for international solidarity and oversight through the RLS or any other mechanism that does not attempt to usurp the role of unions. This is not a frivolous concern: I once heard Kathie Lee Gifford say that the factories at which her signature line of clothes were made had to follow her code of conduct and therefore there was no need for unions. We should be pushing for freedom of association, for example, through codes of conduct and subsequent monitoring. But once that core labor right exists in a country, we should recognize that it is the role of unions to use their power (with international support, if requested) to ratchet up standards—to organize for higher wages, expanded benefits, and so on. In this way, codes of conduct can support the growth and power of unions, but they cannot and should not be seen as a substitute for unions, in China or elsewhere.

3. Environment or Labor?

Is a labor code enough? Interestingly, the authors—at least some of whom have environmental expertise—focus on a labor code of conduct. And, indeed, the work on corporate codes of conduct to date has been far too split, with work on labor issues, on the one hand, and separate work on environmental issues. The challenge, however, is to merge the two. In my view, work on advancing labor rights and standards through corporate codes is the more advanced of the two, given the existence of ILO-delineated core labor rights. We need a multilateral effort to delineate core environmental rights such as the "right to know." And then the challenge is for proposals and campaigns to more consistently merge social and environmental issues.

4. Who Should Be the Umpire?

Do we really want to give the World Bank new life—and an expanded mission—given its poor performance in reducing the economic, environmental, and social havoc that its loans often leave in their wake? Many of our allies in the campaign to change the global economy have spent decades campaigning against the World Bank; we will lose these groups and individuals (especially in the Third World) as supporters of broader corporate accountability if we disparage their decades of work. If we need a global umpire, I suggest we look not to the Bank, but instead to a reformed United Nations (including the ILO), which is potentially the most egalitarian of the international institutions.

5. REGULATORY OR VOLUNTARY?

A major test of a proposal is its ability to move beyond "easier" countries and "better" companies in "easier" sectors. Thus far, the momentum for codes of conduct, for example, has largely been in the apparel, footwear, and toy sectors, and the codes focus primarily on sweatshop conditions. Campaigns that target corporations with some claim to social responsibility (e.g., Nike, Gap, Levi-Strauss, Starbucks) have been more successful in engaging the company. As the authors suggest, the reality is that the somewhat more socially responsible firms have been targeted since they are more likely to engage. This has led to the current, arguably perverse, situation in which the more responsible (but hardly perfect) companies have "voluntary" codes and thus are more vulnerable to criticism for noncompliance while the more egregious companies without codes have been more likely to escape unscathed. This trap seems inherent to almost any voluntary initiative.

How can the RLS proposal be implemented without falling into this trap? The authors suggest some vague regulation, but it is not clear how firms would be "required" to participate, nor how "sanctions" would work. In fact, the authors allude to weak regulations at best when they say that the World Bank might be willing to participate because it "may see the RLS as a lesser evil to the imposition of a social clause."

By whose authority are the RLS requirements set? Are firm-level incentives really enough to set off a "race to the top"? In addition, there is the "brand-name" recognition problem: How will voluntary attempts ever, for example, expand into sectors with no brand-name recognition, such as automobile parts or paperclips?

Yes, we should work on making a better mousetrap in terms of voluntary schemes—and this may be as far as we can hope to get during Bush II. In the end, though, voluntary codes will be most effective if they help stimulate stronger international regulations such as social clauses, and vice versa.

So, Fung, O'Rourke, and Sabel have started an excellent dialogue. I now look forward to the next round of debate. This is the time for those of us who support more environmentally and socially responsible globalization to work together against a common enemy: corporate-led globalization.

SOME UP, SOME DOWN

Pranab Bardhan

I appreciate the concern that Fung, O'Rourke, and Sabel express for transparency, broad-based participation, yardstick competition, independent monitoring, and coordinated action in the current proliferation of piecemeal, divergent, and arbitrary standards in labor regulations and practices in the international marketplace. I also applaud their sincerity of purpose and good intentions. But I find the purpose rather narrow, and the emphasis partly misplaced—and potentially even harmful to the world's poorest people.

Fung, O'Rourke, and Sabel make a good argument for flexible, locally variable, context-specific labor standards, which is a welcome change from the frequent demand from some activists for pious universal (i.e., rich-country) standards. For example, the authors want to judge the labor practices in a transnational enterprise in Vietnam by comparing them with practices in a similar enterprise in Indonesia, not with those in Europe or North America, at least not initially. But it is not clear why they do not extend the argument for comparison or context-specificity to the rest of the economy in Vietnam, or for that matter in any such poor country. The transnational enterprise in a poor country, for all the horror stories about its working conditions and wage levels that outrage consumers in rich countries, is usually, though not always, an island of *relatively* "decent work" (to use a phrase popular in ILO documents) in an ocean of "indecent" and brutal work conditions in the rest of the economy. If those islands are the "sweatshops" (and they no doubt are by some lofty standards), we have to keep in mind the reality that many of the millions of workers in the rest of the economy are usually banging at the gates of the "sweatshops" for a chance of entry.

Suppose that, with participation of firms, activists, and workers in specific firms, labor standards are "ratcheted up" in line with similar enterprises elsewhere. The result may be improvements for workers inside those enterprises, but one should be wary of the consequences for the much larger number of workers left out. In fact, sometimes the improvements in the tiny "island" may be at the expense of those left floating (or sinking) in the "ocean." Relatively high wages or better working conditions in the transnational enterprise are likely to raise the latter's cost of hiring labor, and thus depress labor demand and job prospects for the rest of the workers.

The workers thus left out are more likely to crowd the inferior job markets, depressing wages and working conditions. For example, child labor banned from internationally certified workplaces may end up in much inferior jobs and occupations (including child prostitution), as casual empiricism as well as the findings of an OXFAM study of displaced child labor in Bangladesh suggest. In India, only 5 percent of child labor is in the international sector; the rest is employed in various parts of the domestic economy. When you abolish child labor in this international sector through commonly adopted comprehensive policies like Ratcheting Labor Standards (RLS), without at the same time doing anything about the displaced children, the glow of moral comfort enjoyed by the consumer in rich countries who scrupulously looks for the "no-child-labor-used" label or certification is largely illusory. Similar is the case in the "no-sweatshop" certification, where a "living wage" and better work conditions for a few workers in the monitored international sector may mean non-living or sub-human wages and work conditions for many elsewhere in the economy.

These criticisms do not imply that RLS is a bad thing. But the approach—in general, any regulatory approach that does not take into consideration what economists call opportunity costs and the enormous side effects for the vast majority of the working poor outside of the regulated facility, as well as the need for compensation to those who are actually or potentially displaced by the regulations—is very narrow and, without these simultaneous other measures, potentially harmful. If the "ethical consumer" of the rich country is prepared to pay more for products where she can feel more comfortable about the process of their production, RLS should be combined with coordinated action to collect the premium paid by the consumer to finance the compensatory measures. The banned child worker should be given adequate scholarships to pay not just for schooling, but for the income foregone by the child's desperately poor family. (A recent program for the rural poor in Mexico, called Progresa, offering scholarships for children, paid to a designated woman in the household, conditional on the children's school attendance, has already been quite successful in reducing child labor.)

In addition, some funds will need to be earmarked for improving the school facilities and making them more attractive or accessible for children. (In India, the number of children of school age who are neither in work nor in school is estimated to be more than three times the number of them in child labor.) An example of the possibility of coordinated action in this general area (regulation plus monitoring plus scholarships and amenities) is provided by the international soccer ball producers' agreement in the mid-1990s, whereby in the city of Sialkot in Pakistan (which is one of the world's largest producers of soccer balls, and used to employ many children for stitching the balls) the transnational sporting goods companies agreed to provide scholarships to the children who lost their jobs, some NGOs were to act as monitoring agencies, and the local government was to provide the schooling facilities. In the case of adult sweatshop labor, RLS has to be combined with some investments in the local community that help not just the workers in the improved facility but those who are outside. This is no doubt much more expensive than implementing a simple RLS, but massaging the conscience of the affluent consumers in an over-whelmingly poor world cannot be that cheap.

One should, however, distinguish between labor prac-tices that involve forced or prison labor and hazardous and unsafe work conditions on the one hand, and other kinds of child labor or sweatshop work or substandard wage rates on the other. (The examples cited by Fung, O'Rourke, and Sa-bel combine the two kinds.) In the former case, I am all in favor of a legal or regulatory approach with appropriate monitoring and enforcement. (In the context of prison la-bor, while one is legitimately outraged by stories about China, let me note in passing that UNICOR, a corporation owned by the United States federal government, operates about one hundred factories with prison labor, sells over 150 products, with total sales of about $500 million in 1995.)

But in the case of uncoerced child labor, sweatshops, and substandard wage rates and working conditions, I'd like the regulatory enthusiasts to take into account some of the side effects (and necessary compensation measures) that I have indicated above. Otherwise they may end up hurting the in-tended beneficiaries.

WISHFUL THINKING

Mark Levinson

Fung, O'Rourke, and Sabel offer a disarmingly simple strategy for strengthening labor standards: Accurately inform consumers, via transparent monitors' reports, about corporate behavior, and as firms compete for customer loyalty the magic of the market will "generate improvements that then 'ratchet' standards upward." No laws need to be passed. No need for brutal fights about worker rights in the global economy.

Despite much that is good—for example, they are right to stress the importance of transparency—their proposal is deeply flawed, and filled with wishful thinking.[1] Their analysis of consumer concern about sweatshops is simplistic. This leads to a misunderstanding of how firms respond to publicity about abusive conditions. They have an overly optimistic view of how monitoring works in practice and, finally, they ignore the crucial question of rights and power.

Let's start with the limits of ethical consumerism. The authors do not understand that consumer demand for good and bad conditions is asymmetric. Firms *do* have a lot to lose if they are seen as sweatshop producers. The demand for goods produced under sweatshop conditions is inelastic. Thus, firms will go to great lengths—join the Fair Labor

Associations (FLA) or Social Accountability International (SA8000), adopt codes of conduct, pay monitors to check their factories, increase their public relations efforts—to avoid being perceived as a sweatshop producer.

What firms *will not do* is grant workers basic rights to organize or change the sweatshop structure of the industry. This is because firms have limited ability to raise prices for products made under good conditions. Consumer demand for worker-friendly products, in contrast to sweatshop-made products, is *elastic:* price increases generate sharp drops in demand. The loss of revenue from consumers unwilling to pay more for a garment produced under good conditions is not offset by those willing to pay more.[2]

The authors present an optimistic view of the relationship between monitors and companies. "Firms confident of their outstanding social performance would seek out the most credible monitoring organizations to verify their accomplishments." Replace the word "credible" with "friendly" and one understands how this works in practice.[3] The companies, the monitors, and the monitoring organization all have an interest in the system being "reasonable" or company friendly: the companies because they are looking for protection against being labeled a sweatshop producer; the monitoring organization because they want to attract companies; the monitors because they want the companies to hire them.

* * *

Another example of wishful thinking is the account of how RLS could come into existence. One of the existing monitoring organizations, according to Fung, O'Rourke, and Sabel, could:

> ... differentiate itself from the others through a focus on transparency and disclosure that breaks with now dominant policies of confidentiality and proprietary knowledge. This innovation, while scaring off some corporations fearful of revealing current practices, would make this organization the most credible, encompassing, and capable social-certification entity. This credibility would allow it to impose significant disclosure requirements on its associated firms and monitors, to rank each of them on their social performance, and to set the terms of open comparison for other firms and monitors.

The problem is that *corporations don't want to disclose*. Whatever minimal disclosure has been achieved is due to Herculean efforts by student anti-sweatshop activists. We will not get further disclosure because monitoring organizations think they can "differentiate" themselves by calling for disclosure. No companies will take part. We could pass a law requiring disclosure—I'm all for it—and the authors hint that it would be necessary. But then we are getting dangerously close to top-down regulation, to which RLS was supposed to be an alternative.

The authors do not address the limits of monitoring schemes in the context of authoritarian countries where workers have no right to organize. It is not an accident that most apparel production takes place in such countries. Without a right to organize, the best code in the world means little. At best, codes do not challenge the laws that deny workers their rights. At worst, they provide cover for corporations operating in such settings.[4]

Fung, O'Rourke, and Sabel might respond by saying that RLS aims "not at establishing a minimum fixed set of core workplace rights, but rather at creating a process that makes workplaces as good as they can be, and better over time, as companies become more capable and nations more developed." "How else," they ask, "can we hope to find effective solutions to the new misery of the global economy?"

One way is to empower workers. That means creating rules for the global economy that protect worker's rights. The importance of this is described by Amartya Sen:

The governmental response to acute suffering often depends on the pressure that is put on it, and this is where the exercise of political rights (voting, criticizing, protesting, and so on) can make a real difference. . . . While this connection is clearest in the case of famine prevention, the positive role of political and civil rights applies to the prevention of economic and social disasters generally . . . To concentrate only on economic incentives (which the market system provides) while ignoring political incentives (which democratic systems provide) is to opt for a deeply unbalanced set of ground rules.[5]

The institutions and agreements that govern the global economy (the WTO, NAFTA, World Bank, IMF) operate according to a deeply unbalanced set of ground rules that protect property rights but not human rights. RLS does not challenge those ground rules. That is its fatal weakness. Human rights, as Sen argues, are not a reward of development. Rather, they are critical to achieving it.

THE VIEW FROM THE TROPICS

KAUSHIK BASU

On the face of it there should be nothing contentious about the international labor standards movement. It is meant to be a global effort to raise the working conditions and living standards of workers, primarily in developing countries. What is curious is that the biggest opposition to labor standards has come from its alleged beneficiaries—to wit, Third World workers, unions, and governments. The fear in the South is that once such a global monitoring scheme is brought into existence, it will get diverted into an instrument of protection for the North. In the name of international labor standards, arbitrary and inflexible trade sanctions will be imposed on Third World countries. This fear gets heightened if the labor standards are imposed through the World Trade Organization (WTO), via a "social clause" provision, which would allow the WTO to use trade sanctions against any nation that violates minimal labor standards.[1] The other concern stems from the adjective "international," which suggests a uniform global standard for all nations.

Fung, O'Rourke, and Sabel have come up with an ingenious suggestion for international labor standards that gets around some of these criticisms. They christen this contribution "Ratcheting Labor Standards" (RLS). They try to bring in flexibility by keeping labor standards away from formal global organizations. Instead, they propose a system of collecting and publicizing information about the labor practices of firms, and encouraging consumers, journalists, and other ordinary citizens to use social sanctions, such as product boycott and public criticism, against firms that violate minimal standards. In addition, they recommend that the minimal standards that monitors seek and publicize be different across different nations, depending on their levels of economic development.

I believe that Fung, O'Rourke, and Sabel air the right concerns and steer the debate in the right direction. Nevertheless, I think that, as a practical proposal, RLS is flawed. It will not attain the objectives that the authors (rightly) uphold.

One novel and attractive aspect of their scheme (though this is left latent in their statement) is that they place the burden of responsibility on the firm that violates labor standards, rather than the country where the labor standard is violated. We know from economic analysis in other areas that responsibility, no matter where it is initially placed, can be partly deflected. But holding the firm responsible will have the advantage of the firm not being able to *freely* play one poor nation against another and thus drive down standards.

The main weakness of RLS is rooted in its relying so heavily on social sanctions and citizen action. Such a policy has a nice, progressive ring to it, and a certain kind of flexibility—but its shortcomings outweigh these advantages. First, this will handicap small producers. Consider the soccer ball industry in Pakistan. Soccer balls used to be stitched by thousands of small producers, working out of their homes, which doubled as residence and factory. Even if such a production unit did not use child labor, there would be no way for it to "prove" this to outside monitors. A large producer, on the other hand, can easily centralize production in a big factory, stop children from entering the premises, and prove to outside monitors that production is free of child labor. Indeed, Reebok has done just that in Pakistan. Hence, a by-product of this scheme is that it creates a competitive advantage for large firms by making it virtually impossible for small producers to get certification.

Second, once information on firms is collected and publicized and citizens are encouraged to take action, there is no way of ensuring that this system will achieve the right kind of flexibility. In several domains of our civic life, social sanctions play a useful role. But social sanctions have also been the basis of witch-hunts and the persecution of harmless behavior that happens to deviate from the mainstream. Once consumers in a rich country are given the moral responsibility to enforce standards and they are told that in Ethiopia workers are paid ninety cents for a day's work, it is easy for the consumers to believe that this is not a living wage and begin a boycott of Ethiopian goods, unmindful of the fact that such a boycott could cause unemployment and drive the incomes of many workers down to zero. As Joan Robinson, the eminent British radical economist, once noted, in some situations what is worse for a worker than being exploited is not being exploited.

Also, in a world of informal control, citizens may have biased information. Corporations will soon be competing by deliberately using adverse publicity against firms that sell cheap.

It is not surprising that, while all societies rely on informal mass action for curbing a variety of undesirable actions, there are also domains where we prefer to use more centralized methods for addressing issues of justice—for instance, through the courts. I would argue that labor standards do not belong to the first category; they must not be enforced through informal mass action.

Does this mean that we must take institutional (this includes "governmental") action for raising labor standards? Before answering this, note first that not doing so does not mean that labor standards will necessarily be abysmal. As productivity and wages rise, workers can demand higher standards and have many of these demands met, not through government action but by virtue of the standard forces of the market—namely, the implicit threat that the worker will not otherwise accept the job. Very few people, however, argue that all labor standards should be left to what workers can achieve through market mechanisms. Most countries have laws against workplace sexual harassment, for example; they do not leave it to workers to ensure that they are not harassed by threatening to quit if they are. Likewise, there is reason for public action in certain domains of labor standards in developing countries. The question is: How can this be ensured without hurting the very workers that this is meant to help (by causing unemployment or by impoverishing further an already-poor nation)?

In the debate on international standards, so much attention has been directed at the alleged (and largely unsubstantiated) conflict of interest between First and Third World workers that the tension among workers in different nations of the Third World is often overlooked.[2] In this age of mobile global capital, it is easy for corporations to move their capital from one nation to another. Each developing country hesitates to take action to raise its labor standards for fear of driving capital away to another developing country. Hence, there is need for collective action on labor standards *among the Third World nations.*[3] If we take this seriously, then we need to allow Third World nations to develop their own agenda—a consensus from the tropics—of what constitutes minimal labor standards.

The trouble with the WTO is that it is viewed by most developing nations—not entirely without reason—as an entity controlled by rich nations. Even though it runs on the principle of one-country-one-vote, the "green room" where the agenda is set is, in practice, controlled by industrialized nations. There is a great need to encourage the reorganization of international organizations so that they represent the interests of all nations democratically, and to provide a forum where poor countries can develop their own agenda for what constitutes labor standards.

Action for international labor standards is desirable, and such action must be carried out through global institutions, not informal mass action. But if the institutions do not have democratic representation, the process can work to the detriment of the developing nations. Hence, while we strive toward this goal of global action, we should also be prepared for the possibility that, given the current structure of global governance, we may for the time being prefer to resist globalization in this one area and leave labor-standards policy and intervention to individual nations. It is sobering to recall that in the United States the attempt to bring all states under a common labor code was on the agenda for decades (actively from 1906) before it could finally be implemented in the form of the Fair Labor Standards Act in 1938.

UNIONS AND THE STATE

David Moberg

The proposal for "Ratcheting Labor Standards" (RLS) is a sophisticated elaboration of trends in corporate codes of conduct and private monitoring of workplaces that have developed over the past decade. It would certainly strengthen such monitoring, which has played a problematic but important role in the development of a global movement against sweatshops, and could improve some working conditions.

But ultimately the proposal steers that movement in the wrong direction. It builds on current conditions, which reflect the weakness in this era of globalization of the historic forces for improving workers' conditions—labor unions and state regulation. There is an important role for consumer pressure, pressure from nongovernmental organizations, and even independent monitoring, but it should be to strengthen unions and governmental regulation, not replace them with what ultimately would be a relatively weak, inadequate, and privatized regulatory system.

Fung, O'Rourke, and Sabel argue that a new system of regulation is needed because of problems with uniform standards (which they automatically but unjustifiably link to protectionism) and because the nature of production has changed, with decentralized global chains of production extending into the informal sector. But some uniform standards are legitimate, whatever the level of development. Certainly core International Labor Organization (ILO) standards of the right to organize and prohibition of child or forced labor or racial discrimination are relatively uniform and not protectionist—despite gripes from some politicians in developing countries. Does prohibition of exposure to toxic workplace chemicals have to await a higher level of economic development?

Wages should in some way reflect the development of a country, but a requirement that countries enforce reasonable minimum or living wage standards based on their development would not be protectionist. In any case, the companies in question are not struggling efforts run by entrepreneurs in poor countries hoping to break into a world market. These are operations run by major multinationals, like Nike, based in countries with a very high standard of development that are taking advantage of desperate workers in poor countries. If, as they claim, they are raising living standards in those countries, they can be held to higher standards than domestic industries in those countries. They can afford to pay for higher standards and so can their customers.

Who sets the standards? The authors suggest that firms "would be required to adopt a code of conduct"—but what code? And who would do the requiring? Individual governments could both require and set such standards—like adherence to core labor rights—as the basis for imports, but that would run up against World Trade Organization prohibitions on regulating production methods. The alternative is to make basic labor standards integral to international law and institutions governing trade and to strengthen institutions, such as the ILO. Even the Organization for Economic Cooperation Development (OECD) could develop mandatory codes of conduct for multinationals based in OECD countries.

Although production and ownership of factories has become decentralized, ultimate control over the global chain of production has become ever more centralized. Consumers and governments may not know where every part of every product they buy was made, but people who control corporations do—or they can know if they want to. Indeed, the key to restoring more traditional, effective regulation is to make those dominant corporations legally responsible for every infraction of labor rights at every stage of production, even if they are not the owner and direct employer in every workplace. They do have the power to determine conditions of their contractors and subcontractors. They should be required to make full disclosure of their production chain— that is, to be fully "transparent"—and they should be subject to meaningful penalties for all violations. Because of the internal management systems they already have, as the authors describe, they are capable of enforcing good standards. The authors' reference to the "hot cargo" provisions of

American law and the leverage government gets through penalties on the ultimate controlling corporation illustrates how it is possible to regulate global chains of production.

Any good global regulatory system should emphasize both transparency and sanctions, as the authors propose. But there is reason to be skeptical about their mechanisms of competition and continuous improvement. Ultimately, they rely on "social and market pressures" as the power behind their regulatory system, not the authority of the state (and the quasi-state institutions on a global level) or the power of organized workers. They imagine that social pressures will lead monitors and firms to compete to ever-higher standards in order to appeal to ethical consumers. But history suggests that monitors—like today's financial auditors—will feel strong pressure to collaborate with businesses that employ them and that corporations will be motivated to do only what little they must in order to avoid bad publicity. (There are also many industries that are not very vulnerable to ethical consumer pressures.) If Fung, O'Rourke, and Sabel truly believed their model, they would not endorse any kind of governmental regulatory system—which is precisely what conservatives in this country want by dismantling occupational safety and health, environmental, and other enforcement, though not because they expect an ever-rising standard for corporate conduct.

Social and market pressures can be valuable, but there are limits to the power of the ethical consumer, even one who is fully informed by a new monitoring system. In any case, both workers in unions and ethical consumers would gain power by cooperating, not by posing as alternatives. Despite the authors' insistence on listening to workers' views (who will be listening and deciding?), it is disconcerting that they think that unions, as an afterthought, might compete with nongovernmental monitors to see who does the better job. Shouldn't workers, as a matter of fundamental right, be actively supported in organizing themselves? If a monitor finds that the union isn't succeeding, workers can use the monitor's information to strengthen their hand in dealing with their employer.

There may be a role for nongovernmental organizations and independent monitors, but it is as a way of moving toward and then strengthening real protections of worker interests through governmental regulation and unions, not by creating a privatized, weak system that would take their place.

EDUCATING WORKERS

HEATHER WHITE

Verité (Verification in Trade and Export) is a nonprofit organization that has in the last five years conducted human rights inspections of over six hundred factories in fifty countries. I started Verité six years ago for the purpose of increasing corporations' accountability for labor practices at their subcontracting suppliers' factories. Our programs in factories, which include health and safety improvements and training seminars on women's issues, have been delivered throughout Central America and Asia. Since March 2000, we have been conducting an in-factory worker training program in China that includes basic literacy and math skills, as well as training in labor rights and a variety of issues faced by young women who have migrated to rural areas to work in an urban manufacturing environment. The purpose of these programs is to address what we have identified as an urgent need for workers: to understand their legal rights and protections under local law. We regularly find that workers do not know the basis for their wages. The majority work according to a piece-rate system that conveniently avoids transparency and obscures all information regarding wage calculations with factory management.

Contract workers working in foreign countries are especially vulnerable to wage exploitation and overtime abuses.

In addition to the initiatives proposed by Fung, O'Rourke, and Sabel, I would like to propose a global worker education initiative in all developing countries that produce for Western markets. Until workers are in a position to advocate for themselves, possessing complete knowledge of their legal rights and entitlements, they will be overly dependent on outside auditors to initiate improvements in the workplace, which may or may not happen.

The health and safety issue is somewhat easier to address. In our audits, Verité has found health and safety problems to be among the most common, and in most cases they are relatively straightforward and inexpensive to remedy. Health and safety violations often occur due to management's lack of awareness of local regulations or of best-practice methods that minimize hazards.

Many factories that we have audited have expressed strong interest in upgrading their health and safety programs, but they readily admit they lack the knowledge to do so. We have seen that United States and European companies can have significant impact on working conditions by requiring their business partners to change as a precondition to future orders, and then following through to see whether improvements have been made.

HUMAN DEVELOPMENT

Guy Standing

If we believe in standards of decency, we should deplore
atrocious working conditions and the absence of worker
rights and security, whether in Bangladesh, China, or the
United States, in a Nike plant or a shantytown repair shack.
But *what* should count as standards? And *whose* standards
should be the yardstick?

The ILO was established to set standards, and has produced a huge body of conventions and recommendations.
Unlike many countries, the United States has hardly ratified
any of them. Some might suggest this is not a very good example, especially given the rhetoric devoted to the subject in
the United States. Recently, the ILO passed a Declaration
of Fundamental Principles and Rights, which established
seven core standards to which member countries must sub-
scribe. Some of us inside the ILO worry whether this will
set a floor or a ceiling. But such instruments raise numerous
questions about commitment, implementation, attainment,
progress, and the definition of "best practices." Of course,
analysts and activists give their own answers to such questions, and one can be confident that the authors of "Realizing Labor Standards" have theirs. Still, they must be given,
because there is no easy consensus.

Let me declare an interest. Over the past twenty years, I have conducted surveys of labor practices covering thousands of firms in over twenty countries, including developing countries such as Malaysia, Chile, and the Philippines, and crashing ex-communist countries such as Russia and Ukraine. To convince someone like me, proposals such as Ratcheting Labor Standards (RLS) must satisfy a realism test based on recollections of visits to factories, estates, and mines.

I recall visiting a U.S. multinational in a Malaysian export-processing zone. It was exposing thousands of teenage women to conditions that the manager readily admitted were causing long-term health problems. The conditions were legal. The firm operated where independent unions were banned. Apologists say that conditions and pay in such firms are better than in the surrounding *kampongs*. But what could stop such practices? Nearby, in a back street of Kuala Lumpur, I talked to a Chinese furniture maker. Men, women, and children scurried in and out of the sprawling building. On one definition, he had fifty people working for him; he told me, truthfully, that he had just two doing so.

The U.S. firm had better pay and conditions, but was unnecessarily opportunistic. The Chinese businessman would have melted into the city had inspectors come after him. In both cases, what was lacking was the voice of the workers, which was needed to pressure managers to make feasible changes and to give them knowledge of what to do.

Another lesson from our surveys is that distinctions between "formal" and "informal" sectors make no sense. Informalization has spread everywhere, including within so-called formal enterprises.[1] This means that formalistic monitoring can only relate to a small part of the economy. Contrary to what is suggested in "Realizing Labor Standards," there is little evidence that stable relationships between "producers" and "suppliers" are the norm. With flexible practices, statutory regulations and monitoring procedures are harder to operate than with mass production or when production is less dispersed. A heavy-handed strategy to ratchet up standards would be ineffectual. We must avoid a mixed image in our minds—sickening labor practices in a well-regulated economy. Go to the *favelas* of Sao Paulo or the lanes in the slums of Ahamedebad, where labor relations are harder to monitor than implied by the authors.

Fung, O'Rourke, and Sabel might retort that they are concerned with firms linked to global production, and that a strategy to curb some practices would be better than nothing. They must answer two standard objections. First, the effect could be subject to the law of unintended consequences—that is, it could make matters worse, perhaps by driving practices underground. Second, the cost could be excessive relative to the effect; for example, funds could do more good if just given to vulnerable workers so that they could bargain better, or opt out. Proponents of RLS should answer these points.

* * *

RLS is vague on principles, although "sanctions" and "transparency" are called principles. Surely, the basic principles of RLS should be equity, equality, democracy, and accountability. The biggest difficulty is defining what are good practices, and then "best" practices. For example, there is no law in the United States to allow workers a toilet break when needed. This is rarely on any list of bad practices.

Labor standards are normative, and are a package or nothing. In developing a strategy, you need to identify a core of standards that are a floor of human decency; then practices that accord with a country's capacities and a firm's size and structure; and then standards that are reasonable aspirations. The principles have to be spelled out before any system of monitoring can be assessed, and in RLS this is left vague.

RLS puts heavy emphasis on regulations, monitoring, and sanctions. There is a smell of the big stick, with firms "required to adopt a code of conduct and to participate in a social monitoring program." There are "certifying agencies," "regulatory agencies," and "umpire organizations," as well as "compliance monitoring agreements" and "third-party social auditing." The language is at best paternalistic. We are told the RLS would use "public power," and that "firms that fail to disclose their labor outcomes or monitoring methods should be presumed to have something to hide, and be punished." This is out of step with the time, where incentives to good practice are more likely to elicit support.

There is also a moral hazard in the proposals. We are told, "A firm would select a monitor from among NGOs or auditing companies who provide this service." How cozy. One reads of consultancy firms offering themselves as "social inspectors." Do they have a track record of being advocates of labor standards? It is not their business; they are privileged corporations. The authors do not address how to make NGOs and auditors *accountable*. Who appoints these social auditors? Unless you are a paternalist, democracy should be uppermost—workers' voice should be at the forefront. It should bring a wry smile to read that firms "would seek out the most credible monitoring organizations to verify their accomplishments." I bet they would, and pay them well.

This leads back to basics. What is a good firm? Through our surveys at the ILO, data exist with which to develop company-level indexes of good labor standards in the spheres of skill development, social equity, work security, economic equity, and economic democracy. These are combined into a Human Development Enterprise Index (HDE), ranked on a scale of zero to 25. There are measures of principles (preferences of management, etc.), processes (existence of mechanisms to give effect to principles), and outcomes.

The composite index has been measured for thousands of firms in several countries, and the results show that firms with high scores on what amount to good standards do better economically than those with low scores. There are reasons why this does not lead to all firms adopting good HDE practices. However, if firms were examined to determine whether or not they are pursuing practices associated with high HDE scores, a strategy could be devised to give HDE awards for exemplary firms. This would entitle firms to label their products, advertise as good performers, and receive preference in government contracts.

One reason for an incentive-based awards scheme rather than a sanctions-based campaign is that firms want to identify themselves as good employers, whereas they will try to disguise themselves—or go for gestures and fancy ads, as have the oil companies—if identified as bad. Consumers are unlikely to know about bad firms when they go to shops, whereas the good firms could have a label which they would wish to display.

Here's another trick. Representatives of developing countries claim that linking labor standards to trade amounts to protectionism by rich countries. Yet, if advocates really want global standards they must prevent the erosion of standards in affluent countries. There is no race to the bottom, but one to something like the middle. Attention should be given to the need to retain labor standards, and strong sanctions should be reserved for countries and firms cutting them. Which is worse, a firm or country not raising standards or one that lowers them? Under Pinochet, Chile cut standards, persecuted labor leaders, and then, once workers' organizations were enfeebled, allowed modified freedom of association. The crime came with the cut in standards. The fear is that zealous monitors would concentrate on the final liberalization.

The same applies to the nonsense about labor "deregulation." There has been no labor deregulation (a contradiction in terms), merely a shift from pro-collective to pro-individualistic regulations, and a rolling back of protections so as to reduce "labor costs." When RLS proponents focus on developing countries, and matters such as child labor, they should also look at reforms in affluent countries that lower standards, and of companies that roll back practices that had benefited workers. Perhaps, we should be seeking ways of preventing the ratcheting *down* of standards.

Other dilemmas raised by RLS include the sanguine expectation that the World Bank should play a leading role. Many Bank publications oppose minimum wages in developing countries, and are hostile to unions. Some NGOs depend on Bank contracts, and cease to be independent. The RLS authors reach out to the Bank. But it should remain a bank, and not become embroiled in matters for which it has neither mandate nor competence.[2] It should not be a standards-setter or monitor.

Another worry is that many of us remember feeling lonely when U.S. organizations were silent on these issues, and wonder whether current interest in improving standards is primarily a result of fears about jobs and production shifting to developing countries. Also, to what extent should companies be held accountable for the practices of suppliers, purchasers, and subcontractors? If "monitors" do not like a given law, should a firm be expected to abide by it or to some "higher" standard?

While subscribing to the objectives of the authors of RLS, I have become convinced that incentives to improved practices, combined with public advocacy, have more prospect of success than complex monitoring and sanctions. Above all, though, strengthening the voice of working communities—not putting faith in social auditors—is the most effective way to make substantial progress.

MONETIZE LABOR PRACTICES

IAN AYRES

Is it possible to contract for profit with poor people without being labeled an exploiter? Can you rent to the poor without being a slumlord? Can you lend to the poor without charging usurious interest? Can you hire the poor without running a sweatshop?

Of course, if the terms are fair, contracting with the poor can be a good thing. But how are we to know whether a particular relationship is fair? In the absence of good information about the terms of trade, we tend to think that profiting from contracts with poor people is presumptively bad. We infer abuse from the background characteristics of poverty and profit.

But an irrefutable inference can be pernicious. If an employer who hires poor people is going to be vilified as running a sweatshop regardless of what she does, then what incentive does she have to do the right thing?

So we may be caught in an unhappy equilibrium. In the absence of better information, consumers rationally worry that products manufactured for profit in desperately poor countries are unclean. But manufacturers have no credible mechanism to give them better information: anything the manufacturers say is bound to be treated as suspect.

The "Ratcheting Labor Standards" (RLS) idea espoused by Fung, O'Rourke, and Sabel shows promise in mitigating this problem. By providing consumers with a metric of labor conditions assessed by independent auditors, RLS might be able to foster competition in the fair treatment of labor. Knowing that improved working conditions would be reported to consumers by credible monitors, manufacturers would have an incentive to make improvements. So RLS could provoke a race toward the top instead of toward the bottom.

I worry, however, about the authors' emphasis on "continuous improvement" and "ratcheting." If manufacturers correctly sense that nothing they do will ultimately prove sufficient, they will be less willing to cooperate with the institution of RLS. The notion of what would constitute fair working conditions is not adequately defined, but seems to be ever-expanding. For example, to avoid a charge of exploitation, Microsoft could not simply say that it was paying more than the going rate in the country, and that there was excess demand for its jobs—because under RLS the core comparisons seem to be across countries. Meanwhile, under the "continuous improvement" principle, even a manufacturer who shows that it paid more that manufacturers in similar countries might not be in the clear for long. The authors intend to keep ratcheting up the standards. Their proposal eschews any safe harbor.

I also worry that as currently articulated the RLS standards are too mushy to provide consumers with much credible information. In rating a facility, the faithful monitor is supposed to compare the treatment of workers in different developing countries and to heed the "voice of the workers." The monitor's Delphic pronouncements of "good" or "bad" would have little falsifiable content. This puts too much pressure on the legitimacy of the monitor and the monitor's monitor. But these monitors might themselves be captured by political as well as industrial interests. If confidence in the monitoring system declines, however, then we are back to square one: consumers do not know what to believe, and manufacturers consequently lose the incentive to make improvements.

My friendly amendment is that RLS should strive to monetize labor practices. Specifically, firms that disproportionately manufacture in developing countries should be encouraged to disclose point-of-purchase information about the average hourly labor costs of manufacturing particular goods. A consumer poised to buy a Timberland shoe might be willing to buy a more expensive brand upon learning that the employees had only been paid 22 cents per hour.

Money is the quintessential metric of value. While it is difficult to monetize the quality of housing that a landlord provides, the most important part of an employer's treatment of labor is already monetized—that is, the employee's wage. Of course, it would be necessary to monetize other aspects of an employer's labor practices. Employers who provide health care should be able to monetize these labor costs as well as the nominal wage. And an adjustment for long hours might be implemented by discounting (by a third) the wages of those who work more than forty hours a week.

Some labor practices, however, are resistant to the monetization approach. Occupational safety risks would be more difficult to assess, although for large enough or long-enough-lived enterprises, such as Pou Chen, it might be possible to monetize the historical accident rate.

But it is probably better to leave the metric slightly under-inclusive but more transparent for the harried consumer. Disclosing the average hourly labor costs of products still gives consumers a highly probative summary statistic of how well labor is treated. The essential point is that consumers think the information is reliable, and that they know how to interpret it. Providing consumers with labor cost information also allows them to make an informed judgment about whether they are willing to pay more for a fairer wage. Instead of the a priori imperative that standards continuously improve, a neutral disclosure regime would cast the consumer as the ethical sovereign determining what level of compensation is fair. Indeed, one could even imagine a disclosure regime that lead toward a ratcheting down—if consumers felt that some workers were being paid an unfairly high wage (say, relative to the wage of the consumer herself).

Ben and Jerry's tried an imperfect version of wage disclosure for a number of years, pledging for a time that its highest paid employees would earn no more than seven times the salary of its lowest-paid full-time employee. While the salary pledge was insufficiently inclusive (excluding the value of executives' stock and options), the central idea of providing consumers with a falsifiable numeric claim has merit.

Each year, law students pour over the form resumes that law firms fill out to recruit students. The forms require the firms to describe their attitude toward pro bono activities and the firms invariably (and thus uninformatively) report that they such work is "strongly encouraged." Now, one approach consistent with RLS would be to have independent monitors undertake multifaceted analysis of a firm's pro bono practice. But to my mind, it would be better to ask firms to report the average number of pro bono hours provided by attorneys in the firm. This is a more minimalist system that is more likely to encourage the kind of ethical competition that is really the core contribution of the RLS idea.

3

REPLY

ARCHON FUNG, DARA O'ROURKE, AND CHARLES SABEL

Ratcheting Labor Standards (RLS) is a proposal about how to achieve worker rights. It relies on methods of monitoring and enforcement that seem dubious from the standpoint of centralized rule-making. So it is perhaps no surprise that many of our critics have responded skeptically. Nevertheless, we maintain that advancing workers' rights, broadly conceived, requires enlisting the energies of consumers, NGOs, auditing firms, workers, and individual corporations.

RLS, like other labor standards strategies, assumes first that workers have the right to decent treatment—for the same reasons they have human rights. Second, and more contentiously, RLS assumes that little is achieved, and much may be jeopardized, by defining human rights of labor too narrowly, and then entrusting the enforcement of "core" rights to existing international organizations. Third, its distinctive hope is that something like the protections that a traditional rights regime promises, but seldom delivers, can be reached through a new route: a system of decentralized but linked efforts to improve labor standards that in effect reveals what we mean by human rights at work as we learn how to implement them in different settings. Thus, RLS aims to fill the gap between the promise and performance of the rights agenda, not to substitute for it.

Some of our critics, rejecting the second assumption, overlook the defects of traditional rights views. David Moberg and Robin Broad are the most ardent advocates of a clear, universal set of minimum human rights at work that apply to all nations and firms, because, as Moberg writes, "some uniform standards are legitimate, whatever the level of development." As Broad and Moberg argue, the effectiveness of such codes depends on building wide consensus around a small set of what are deemed core rights. To achieve consensus on rights, however, sharp lines must be drawn between covered and uncovered areas. Within areas covered by rights, there are then crisp distinctions between acceptable and unacceptable conduct. But these distinctions are arbitrary except from the point of view of the political battles to achieve consensus. Moreover, determined firms can easily escape the discipline of its code. And nothing in the process of reaching consensus, or enforcing a code of rules, fosters movement to improve labor standards themselves.

Thus, as Heather White observes, health and safety problems are widespread, very important to workers, and often relatively easy to fix. Yet health and safety seldom appears on lists of "core" rights. Discrimination, which is not manifestly more (or less) widespread, onerous to employees, or difficult to fix, is. Moberg himself is aware of this sort of

problem: He would like living, or at least minimum, wages
to be part of a consensus on basic labor rights, but the idea is
too controversial to survive the exclusionary razor of international consensus. The same arbitrariness plagues such basic rights as freedom of association. Very generally speak-
ing, OECD countries are better at respecting this basic
right than developing countries. But there are important
differences within the "advanced" group. Indeed, Human
Rights Watch last September reported widespread violations of the rights to organize in the United States.[1] Among
developing countries the differences are at least as great as
between the United States and, say, Austria. Countries like
China and El Salvador severely restrict this freedom, while
India is more respectful of it. If a bright line separates countries that respect the right to freedom of association from
those that don't—and without such a line there cannot be a
code of core rights—on which side does the United States
fall? India? The three best factories in China? Its three
worst?

Such ambiguities invite wrongdoers to make a sham of
compliance. To silence international outcry, a dictator
might stop assassinating labor leaders (a plain violation of
freedom of association) and instead intimidate workers by
organizing them into official unions controlled by his son-
in-law (a practice not so easy to categorize). A company that
doesn't want to be denounced for discrimination can recover
what it spends on, say, treating men and women equally, by
cutting back expenditures on health and safety.

Finally, at their very worst, bright-line rules sometimes "solve" labor problems while imperiling the people the rights were meant to protect. This is the result, as we know from the work of Kaushik Basu and others, in cases such as child labor, where uniform prohibitions and sanctions can push children out of factories into prostitution, and deny their families crucial incomes.

These observations on the limits of minimal rights are hardly original to us. Several of the respondents, in fact, recognize the weaknesses of strategies based on bright-line rights and uniform standards. But the remedies they offer seem almost a fig leaf for despair, rather than the foundations for a robust alternative.

Guy Standing, for example, worries that the declaration of core standards by the International Labor Organization (ILO) will create a ceiling rather than a floor for the development of worker rights. He is aware of the mismatch between sharp lines and complex reality. (The elaborate system of classification of labor conditions of which he speaks, however, is a research project, not an operating system; and it is more likely to encourage debate of the kind that RLS aims to provoke and systematize than to resolve matters once and for all.) We share, as should be obvious from the design of RLS itself, his concern for the possibility of collusion between monitors and those being monitored.[2] But we simply don't follow his conclusion that a system based solely on incentives will do better than our carrot-and-stick public-accountability approach. Wouldn't the honest application of incentives also require social monitoring?

Ian Ayres is also aware of the complexity of the regulatory problem. Indeed, he worries that any system, RLS included, that tries to take this complexity fully into account will suffer from information overload. To reduce institutional burdens to manageable proportions he suggests monetizing labor standards by basing them on wages and benefits. The great danger, as he acknowledges, is that crucial areas such as health and safety are neglected because costs and benefits are hard to monetize. For this reason it is unlikely that his solution will find much support, except as a very chastened second-best. RLS is a way to develop metrics that incorporate additional dimensions of worker welfare, monetizable and not. As to the information overload problem in general: experiences in other regulatory areas noted in our piece suggest that RLS-type systems both need and supply much more information than traditional ones, and often develop the institutional machinery necessary to effectively process that information.

Pranab Bardhan argues that RLS has troubles dealing with unintended consequences, and especially the problem of boundaries and spillover effects between firms in the "informal" and "formal" sectors. We agree that this is a large difficulty for RLS. However, we have reason to think that RLS will respond better to these problems than other regulatory strategies. First, we believe that the same principles of transparency, comparison, and competition would be useful in continuously improving labor standards in the informal sector, though the institutions would obviously differ from those designed to regulate multinationals and their suppliers. Second, RLS is an open system in which parties are encouraged to raise new concerns as relevant dimensions of social performance. We would expect NGOs and other groups to raise objections to allegedly successful programs and regulations in RLS on account of their spillover effects on the informal sector or other unintended consequences. Once raised, successive innovations would have to account for these no longer unintended impacts in order to earn high marks.

For example, the ILO and many others now recognize that developing a humane—and sane—approach to realizing children's rights require careful, coordinated, pro-active experimentation with strategies such as compensatory measures and integrated programs. Unlike bright-line rights and their enforcement institutions, RLS aims to encourage, evaluate, and diffuse just such constructive exploration.

Because the most successful programs are likely to come from many different kinds of actors, it would be a mistake to assign some a privileged role in developing these solutions and standards. That is why we reject the suggestion of Levinson, Moberg, and Broad that organized labor and traditional regulators can be the only real champions of labor standards. A central aim of RLS is to devise methods to increase space for free association, in part because we expect that worker organizations will often prove to be effective monitors and innovators. But improvements can also come from other quarters—NGOs, informal workers, or even firms themselves. A strategy that recognizes and encourages this diversity does not threaten the cause of labor or the project of regulation, but rather strengthens and complements it. Similarly, we reject Basu's suggestion that labor standards ought to be determined by a "consensus from the tropics." We whole-heartedly endorse developing nations as full participants along with other parties, but disagree that the tropics (especially where governments are not responsive to their citizens) should possess a monopoly on labor standards.

RLS is speculative and incomplete in its formulation—in keeping with its own design principles. We cannot pretend to have answered all of the questions; answers must arise from collaboration between practitioners and observers of regulation. Our original contribution grows out of such collaboration, and it is our hope that this exchange will foster it further.

NOTES

FUNG, O'ROURKE, AND SABEL / *Realizing Labor Standards*

1. Martha Chen, Jennefer Sebstad, and Lesley O'Connell, "Counting the Invisible Workforce: The Case of Homebased Workers," *World Development* 27 (1999): 603–610.

2. David Weil, "Leveraging Time: Regulating U.S. Labor Standards in the Age of Lean Retailing" (Manuscript, 2000).

3. Massachusetts Toxics Use Reduction Program, *Evaluating Progress: A Report on the Findings of the Massachusetts Toxics Use Reduction Program and Evaluation* (Lowell, Mass.: Toxics Use Reduction Institute, March 1997).

4. This account is taken from National Academy of Public Administration, *Environment.Gov: Transforming Environmental Regulation for the 21st Century* (Washington, D.C.: National Academy of Public Administration, 2000).

5. See James T. Hamilton, "Pollution as News: Media and Stock Market Reactions to the Toxics Released Inventory Data," *Journal of Environmental Economics and Management* 28 (Jan 1995): 98–113; "Exercising Property Rights to Pollute: Do Cancer Risks and Politics Affect Plant Emission Reductions?," *Journal of Risk and Uncertainty* 18 (1999): 105–124.

6. US Environmental Protection Agency, *Toxics Release Inventory 1998 Data Release* (Washington, D.C.: USEPA, 2000).

7. World Bank, *The Greening of Industry* (Washington, D.C.: World Bank, 1999).

8. They conducted similar surveys in 1995 and 1996, with similar results. Approximately 1,000 people responded, and the data were weighted to reflect demographic characteristics of U.S. adults ages 18 and

over. Authors report a margin of error at the 95 percent confidence level of plus or minus 3 percent. See http://www.marymount.edu/news/garmentstudy/.

9. Richard B. Freeman, "What Role for Labor Standards in the Global Economy" (12 November 1998).

10. See: http://www.environics.net/eil/ millennium/.

11. Social Investment Forum, *1999 Report on Responsible Investment Trends in the United States,* November 4, 1999.

12. See, for example, *Visions of Ethical Sourcing,* ed. Raj Thamotheram (London: Financial Times Press, 1999).

13. On these audits see, for instance, Dara O'Rourke, "Monitoring the Monitors: A Critique of PricewaterhouseCoopers Labor Monitoring," available at http://web.mit.edu/dorourke/www/.

14. See: http://www.workersrights.org/factory__locations.html.

15. See: http://www.nikebiz.com/labor/index.shtml.

MARK LEVINSON / *Wishful Thinking*

1. One of the greatest weaknesses of the current monitoring programs such as Fair Labor Association and Social Accountability International is the lack of transparency. In contrast, the Workers' Rights Consortium (WRC) is based on transparency. Of all the organizations to arise out of concern about sweatshops, the WRC is the most promising. For an explanation of its "verification model" and an example of transparent reporting, see http://www.workersrights.org.

2. For an analysis of consumer demand for labor standards, see Kimberly Elliott and Richard Freeman, "White Hats or Don Quixotes? Human Rights' Vigilantes in the Global Economy," paper presented to NBER Conference on Emerging Labor Market Institutions (August, 2000). Elliott and Freeman argue that "If consumers responded more to information about good conditions than about bad conditions, activists and firms would have some common ground on which to work."

3. See the devastating critique of SA8000 monitoring in China, "No Illusions: Against the Global Cosmetic SA8000," Labor Rights in China (1999).

4. One reason to be skeptical about existing codes: of 61 factories "certified" by SA8000, 34 of them are in China. In the SA8000 code there is

very strong language about freedom of association. If any workers in those 34 factories were to try and exercise the rights spelled out in the code they would find themselves in jail or an insane asylum.

5. Amartya Sen, "Human Rights and Asian Values," *New Republic,* July 14, 1997.

KAUSHIK BASU / *The View from the Tropics*

1. On this see Jagdish Bhagwati, "Trade Liberalization and 'Fair Trade' Demands," *World Economy* 18 (1995): 745–759.

2. I argue these unsubstantiated instances in "International Labor Standards and Child Labor," *Challenge* 42 (September/October 1999): 80–92.

3. This is formally modeled in my "Child Labor: Cause, Consequence and Cure, with Remarks on International Labor Standards," *Journal of Economic Literature* 37 (1999): 1083–1119.

GUY STANDING / *Human Development*

1. For more information see Guy Standing, *Global Labour Flexibility: Seeking Distributive Justice* (London: Macmillan, 1999).

2. See my article "Brave New Words? A Critique of a World Bank Rethink," *Development and Change* (September 2000).

FUNG, O'ROURKE, AND SABEL / *Reply*

1. Human Rights Watch, "Unfair Advantage: Workers' Freedom of Association in the United States under International Human Rights Standards" (September 2000).

2. We ourselves have written some of the strongest critiques on record of monitoring practices. See O'Rourke, "Monitoring the Monitors," http://web.mit.edu/dorourke/www/.

ABOUT THE CONTRIBUTORS

IAN AYRES is the William K. Townsend Professor at Yale Law School. He is the author of *Pervasive Prejudice?: Unconventional Tests of Race and Gender Discrimination*.

PRANAB BARDHAN is professor of economics at the University of California, Berkeley, and the chief editor of the *Journal of Development Economics*.

MEDEA BENJAMIN is the founding director of Global Exchange, an organization that pressures U.S. corporations to be more accountable to the environment, their workers, and the communities in which they are located. She has been a leading figure in the movements to stop abuses by individual companies such as Nike and Gap, as well as international institutions such as the World Trade Organization.

KAUSHIK BASU is professor of economics and Carl Marks Professor of International Studies at Cornell University. His most recent book is *Prelude to Political Economy*.

ROBIN BROAD, professor of Third World development at American University, is author of *Unequal Alliance: The World Bank and the International Monetary Fund in the Philippines*.

JOSHUA COHEN is professor of philosophy and Sloan Professor of Political Science at the Massachusetts Institute of Technology. He is editor-in-chief of *Boston Review* and author of numerous books and articles in political theory.

ARCHON FUNG is assistant professor at the John F. Kennedy School of Government at Harvard University.

MARK LEVINSON is director of policy and research at the Union of Needletrades, Industrial, and Textile Employees (UNITE) and the book review editor for *Dissent*.

{ 97 }

ABOUT THE CONTRIBUTORS

DAVID MOBERG is senior editor of *In These Times* and a fellow of the Nation Institute.

DARA O'ROURKE is assistant professor in the department of urban studies and planning at the Massachusetts Institute of Technology.

JOEL ROGERS is professor of law, political science, and sociology at the University of Wisconsin, a member of the *Boston Review* editorial board, and author of numerous articles and books on American politics.

CHARLES SABEL is professor of law at Columbia University.

GUY STANDING is director of the socioeconomic security program for the International Labor Organization. This paper is written in a personal capacity; views expressed here should not be attributed to the International Labor Organization.

HEATHER WHITE is executive director of Verité, a nonprofit human rights monitor based in Amherst, Massachusetts.

ML